The War Is Over

God Is Not Mad, So Stop Struggling with Sin and Judgment

by
Andrew Wommack

D. Jean Rawls
1-8-11
January

719-635-1111

Harrison House
Tulsa, Oklahoma

13 12 11 10   10 9 8 7 6 5

The War Is Over:
God's Not Mad, So Stop Struggling with Sin and Judgment
ISBN 13: 978-1-57794-935-0
ISBN 10: 1-57794-935-8
Copyright © 2008 by Andrew Wommack Ministries, Inc.
P.O. Box 3333
Colorado Springs, CO 80934-3333
www.awmi.net

Published by Harrison House Publishers
P.O. Box 35035
Tulsa, Oklahoma 74153
www.harrisonhouse.com

Contents

Introduction

The War Is Over will either make you glad or mad, but you won't be indifferent anymore. Using God's Word, I counter a tremendous amount of religious teaching masquerading as "Christianity" today and establish the truth of the Gospel. Wherever I have taught this message, many people have told me they were shocked at first, but were set free as they meditated on these truths (see John 8:32).

Do you struggle with the fact that God is not angry or upset with you? Have you ever heard or accepted that God loves you in spite of what you do or don't do; that His love for you isn't based on your performance? There needs to be some major changes in the way many Christians believe. The Word clearly reveals that if we aren't getting the right results, it's because we aren't believing right.

As he thinketh in his heart, so is he.

Proverbs 23:7

I understand that there's a resistance to changing the way we think, but it's the way we think that has caused us to be the way we are. Most Christians I've met feel like there's a lot of room for improvement in the way they're receiving from God.

This message could bring the breakthrough in your relationship with God that you so desire—I want to help you become reconciled to (or back in harmony and friendship with) God. So I encourage you not to reject the truths presented in this book just because they sound different. Listen to the Lord, and let Him speak to you. You'll be blessed to know that *The War Is Over!*

CHAPTER 1

Good Will Toward Men

There were in the same country shepherds abiding in the field, keeping watch over their flock by night. And, lo, the angel of the Lord came upon them, and the glory of the Lord shone round about them: and they were sore afraid. And the angel said unto them, Fear not: for, behold, I bring you good tidings of great joy, which shall be to all people. For unto you is born this day in the city of David a Saviour, which is Christ the Lord. And this shall be a sign unto you; Ye shall find the babe wrapped in swaddling clothes, lying in a manger. And suddenly there was with the angel a multitude of the heavenly host praising God, and saying, Glory to God in the highest, and on earth peace, good will toward men.

Luke 2:8–14

This is a familiar passage of scripture. All too often we use it to create a certain mood and get ourselves into the "Christmas spirit." The problem is we don't really think about what this is saying.

Instead of "Glory to God in the highest, and on earth peace, good will toward men," many translations actually render Luke 2:14 to say, "peace among men," or "peace toward men of good-will," or something similar. Since this tends to be the dominant interpretation, most people think that the angels were proclaiming that Jesus' arrival would stop division, end strife, and usher in a new era of peace on earth. They believe that this announcement means that the Lord was coming to bring peace among men. Yet, that's not what this verse is saying.

A Sword

Jesus himself declared:

> Think not that I am come to send peace on earth: I came not to send peace, but a sword. For I am come to set a man at variance against his father, and the daughter against her mother, and the daughter in law against her mother in law. And a man's foes shall be they of his own household.
>
> Matthew 10:34–36

The Lord also prophesied that one of the signs of the end times would be increased war, division, and strife.

> Ye shall hear of wars and rumours of wars: see that ye be not troubled: for all these things must come to pass, but the end is not yet. For nation shall rise against nation, and kingdom against kingdom.... All these are the beginning of sorrows.
>
> Matthew 24:6–8

You simply cannot defend the position that Jesus came to bring peace among people. Now it's true that there are benefits available for those who will receive the Prince of Peace into their heart (see Isa. 9:6). By God's grace, you can turn the other cheek, love your enemies, and operate in a different degree of love (see Luke 6:27–29; 1 Cor. 13). I don't doubt that there has been a tremendous amount of peace among men as a by-product of people receiving salvation—but that's not the message the angels were singing. That's not what Jesus himself said He came here to do.

Jesus Ended the War

What were these angels proclaiming?

Glory to God in the highest, and on earth peace, good will toward men.

Luke 2:14

They were announcing, "Peace. Good will toward men from God!"

Prior to the advent of the Lord Jesus Christ, God was at war against man's sins. His wrath came upon people because of the sin in their lives. Many Christians haven't mentally separated this out and really looked at it. They just run everything in the Bible together. Yet a closer examination of God's Word reveals that there was a wrath and a judgment from God against people in the Old Testament that is totally unjustified and wrong in the New Testament. Why? Jesus ended the war between God and man. He made all the difference!

Despite that, most people run all of this together. They still think of God as being angry at our sins. They mistakenly believe that there is still a war going on between God and man, and that every time they sin, somehow or another it's a new affront against Him. You've probably heard people say, "God is ticked off!" and quote Old Testament scriptures about the wrath of God falling on people. "God is angry today," they insist. "He's dangling our country over hell by a thin thread that's on fire, and He's just about ready to turn us over to the devil." Some Christians are proclaiming that God is the One who sent the hurricanes and tsunamis that have struck in recent years, and that He's going to cause other disasters too. Several well-known religious leaders stood up and declared that God was the One who sent the terrorist attacks that happened in 2001 and that this was the beginning of His judgment on our nation. They're still proclaiming that there is wrath from God towards men.

Good News

Yet, this isn't the message of the New Testament. These angels who announced the birth of Jesus understood the Gospel. They understood that He came to pay the price, to redeem us, and to stop God's wrath upon sin. The New Testament church should be proclaiming to people that their sins have been paid for. We ought to be telling people the Gospel.

The Gospel is good news. In fact, this Greek word translated *gospel* actually means nearly-too-good-to-be-true news.[1] The Gospel is the nearly-too-good-to-be-true news that God isn't angry with you, that He loves you, and that He wants to extend all of His blessings toward you.

As a whole, the church isn't preaching this. We're still telling people that God is angry with them, and then we wonder why they aren't beating down the doors to get into the church. It's the goodness of God that leads people to repentance (see Rom. 2:4).

God is just, but Jesus paid the price. (See 1 Cor. 6:20.) He totally changed the way God deals with mankind. That's what these angels were singing about.

God Isn't Upset

While summarizing the ministry of Jesus, Paul made the same point in the epistle he wrote to the Corinthians.

> Therefore if any man be in Christ, he is a new creature: old things are passed away; behold, all things are become new. And all things are of God, who hath reconciled us to himself by Jesus Christ.
>
> 2 Corinthians 5:17,18

To *reconcile* is simply to make friendly or to bring back into harmony. Can you see that God is not upset with you?

Some of the things I'm about to share run so contrary to our Christian culture that you may be tempted to reject them and lay this book aside. Nevertheless, I'm just going to step out in faith and make some radical statements, trusting that the Holy Spirit will bear witness to you. I pray that you'll read the rest of the book and give me a chance to explain. This could be the breakthrough in your relationship with God that you've been believing for.

God is not upset. In fact, not only is He not mad at you as a Christian—a point that many believers really struggle with—but He's also not mad at unbelievers. God is not about to judge this nation.

Wrath Appeased

I used to preach that if God didn't judge America, He'd have to apologize to Sodom and Gomorrah. Our country is as corrupt—or pretty close to it—as were Sodom and Gomorrah. (See Gen. 13:13; 18:20.) I used to proclaim that until my mind became renewed to God's Word. Now I know that if God were to judge America, He'd have to apologize to Jesus.

Jesus made a difference in the way God relates to mankind. This is what the angels were praising Him for in Luke 2:14. They were really saying, "Glory to God in the highest. The war is over!" The anger and wrath of God has been atoned and appeased. God's wrath was placed upon His Son, and He isn't angry with us anymore.

> All things are of God, who hath reconciled us to himself by Jesus Christ, and hath given to us the ministry of reconciliation.
>
> 2 Corinthians 5:18

The Lord made us friendly. He brought us—not only believers, but all mankind—back into harmony with God. The debt has been paid. Now we must receive it. We must put our faith in the Lord before what He has provided has its full effect in our lives. But God's wrath has been appeased. Man may not be reconciled to God, but God has been reconciled to man. His wrath is over—and He's given us the ministry of reconciliation.

The reason that Christianity isn't having a greater impact on our world than it is today is that we aren't preaching this message.

The Power of God

I am not ashamed of the gospel of Christ: for it is the power
of God unto salvation to every one that believeth.

Romans 1:16

The meaning of the Greek word translated "salvation" here
isn't limited only to the forgiveness of sins. It's also talking about
healing, prosperity, and deliverance—everything Jesus came to
do.[2] Therefore, the power of God for you and me to receive
salvation (forgiveness of sins, healing, prosperity, and deliverance) is released through the Gospel—the nearly-too-good-to-
be-true news—of Jesus Christ.

As a whole, the church isn't preaching this. We're telling
people, "You're going to hell. You're a sinner, and God is angry!"
It's true that before we were born again[3] we were—by nature—
sinners. Our sin separated us from God. Although this is the
truth, it's not "good news." It's not the Gospel.

The Gospel speaks of how God placed all of the punishment
for our sins upon Jesus. In spite of our sins, our relative unworthiness, and need, Christ paid the price for us. Justice demanded
our punishment, but Jesus took it for us. Now God's wrath has
been forever satisfied. He's not angry with people. Jesus paid the
price, and all we must do is receive that payment. That's good
news. That's the Gospel!

Since much of the church isn't preaching the Gospel—the
nearly-too-good-to-be-true news of Jesus Christ—people aren't
coming to the Lord. The power of the Gospel isn't in manifestation much today, and that's why people are turning away from it.

"Not Imputing"

Now, I'm not against the church. I love God's people everywhere. However, very few of them recognize the Gospel—as recorded and expressed in the Word—when they hear it. That's why I usually prefer to hold citywide meetings in a hotel or convention center, rather than in a building called a "church." I've been run out of town, kicked off of radio stations, and removed from television stations for preaching that God isn't mad anymore. Yet, this is the same message the angels proclaimed at Jesus' birth.

> Glory to God in the highest, and on earth peace, good will toward men.
>
> Luke 2:14

They were declaring, "God is not angry. There's peace. He's not upset with you!" In spite of that truth, somehow or another, people today just love to let others know just how "angry" God is, thinking that this will drive them away from hell. That's simply not the way it works.

The Lord has given us the ministry of reconciliation:

> *God was in Christ*, reconciling the world unto himself, *not imputing their trespasses unto them*; and hath committed unto us the word of reconciliation.
>
> 2 Corinthians 5:19

Notice the phrase "God was in Christ...not imputing." This word *impute* means "to hold against."[4] It's actually an accounting term. If you bought something and said, "Put that on my account," they would write it down. Then, at the end of the month, you'd have to pay up. "Not imputing" would be like using a credit card to purchase something, yet it is never charged to your bill. That amount isn't held against you. This verse says that "God was in Christ" not holding man's sins against them.

"Hush Money"

This was the reason that Jesus was so radical. It's why the religious leaders of His day came out against Him. They stayed in power and kept people under their thumb by holding the wrath of God over their heads. They said, "We're the ones who have the truth. If you don't come to our synagogue, give us your tithe, and all these other things, then God will get you!"

It's like the mafia. Guido comes and knocks on your door. He says, "There's sure a lot of arson in this area, and many stores have been broken into. Your business stands a good chance of getting robbed or burned to the ground. But if you pay me, the boys and I will keep that from happening." Of course, Guido and the boys are the ones doing all this, but he wants you to pay them their "hush money."

In a sense, this is what many churches are preaching. "God is angry with you, and He's fixing to get you. But if you will come to church, pay your tithes, read the Bible an hour a day, do this, and do that, then you can appease the wrath of God. Then He won't send your children to the hospital, wreck your marriage, or otherwise destroy your life." I believe that to a large degree the church is like the mafia, saying, "If you'll pay up, if you will keep up on our list of things to do, then God will stay off your case for one more week." That's how they're trying to motivate people to serve the Lord—and wrongly so.

The Word reveals that God was in Christ *not* imputing man's sins unto them. Jesus—both by His life and His message—declared, "God isn't mad at you anymore. Your sins aren't a problem!"

Many Christians would like to stone you for standing up and saying, "Your sin isn't a problem with God." They'll ask, "How could you say such a thing? You're making light of sin. You're acting as though there is nothing wrong with sin." No, that's not what I'm saying. I'm not encouraging anyone to sin. If you just stick with me, I'll be putting all of this into perspective.

Sin Isn't the Issue

Anyone who takes what I'm sharing and says, "This is awesome. I love it! Now I can go live in sin," needs to be born again. The Word declares:

> Every man that hath this hope in him purifieth himself, even as he is pure.
>
> 1 John 3:3

If you are truly born again and have the hope of being like Jesus, then you're looking for a way to overcome sin—not indulge it. If you take what I'm saying and tell people, "Andrew is encouraging people to sin," you're either lying or you've misunderstood what I'm communicating.

When people accuse me of making light of sin, I respond, "You're making light of Jesus!" I'm not saying that sin isn't bad and that you can just go live in it. Sin is terrible, but it's not as big as Jesus. The Lord paid for our sins. (See 1 Cor. 6:20; 7:23.) The payment He made is infinitely greater than the sins of the entire world. One drop of Jesus' blood was more holy, more righteous, more pure than all of the impurity and ungodliness of this entire world put together. When the Lord Jesus Christ died for our sins, His sacrifice forever satisfied the wrath of God. Sin isn't the issue.

CHAPTER 2

Be Reconciled to God

Contrary to popular opinion, people don't go to hell because of their sins. They go to hell because they rejected the payment for their sins. They go to hell because they refused to receive the Savior. When Christians proclaim, "If you don't quit dipping, cussing, chewing, and doing this and that, God won't accept you," you're imputing people's sins unto them. You are also demeaning and decreasing the value of Jesus' sacrifice. In reality, you're saying, "Your sin is bigger and more important than what Jesus did on the cross."

But God was in Jesus not imputing man's sins unto them. Sin isn't the issue. It's all a matter of what people are doing with Jesus. Have they made a commitment of their life to Him, or are they rejecting Him? If someone doesn't receive Jesus as their Savior, they reject the only payment available for their sins. There's no other way to the Father except through His Son.

> Jesus saith unto [Thomas], I am the way, the truth, and the life: no man cometh unto the Father, but by me.
>
> John 14:6

So if they don't accept the payment for their sins—the Lord Jesus Christ—they'll be rejected and cast into hell, not because of their sins, but because of rejecting Jesus. In hell, they'll be held accountable and have to pay for those sins. But the truth is, all those sins have already been paid for by Jesus. Therefore, sin isn't really the issue. The issue is what are you going to do with the Lord?

Receive God's Love

If you have already received the Lord Jesus Christ, then you've been born again. (If you haven't, there's a prayer you can pray at the end of this book.) Sin isn't an issue. God isn't angry with you over your sin. The Lord wants you to stop focusing on sin and start receiving His love. God loves you even though you don't deserve it. He's pleased with you even though you're not pleased with yourself. If you could ever get a picture of the price Jesus paid for your sins, you'd fall head over heels in love with Him. And since faith works by love (see Gal. 5:6), your faith would shoot through the roof!

When you read the Word with this proper mindset, 1 John 5 makes much more sense.

> By this we know that we love the children of God, when we love God, and keep his commandments. For this is the love of God, that we keep his commandments: and his commandments are not grievous.
>
> 1 John 5:2,3

This passage is not saying, "Keep the commandments to get God to love you." It's saying, "If you understood the love of God, you'd keep His commandments. If you truly comprehended just how much Jesus loves you and the price He paid to reconcile you to God the Father, you'd serve Him more accidentally than you ever have on purpose. You'd live holier accidentally motivated by love than you ever have on purpose due to fear and dread. You'd experience a whole new joy and peace in your relationship with God that you've never had before."

> God was in Christ, reconciling the world unto himself, not imputing their trespasses unto them; and hath committed unto us the word of reconciliation.
>
> 2 Corinthians 5:19

This is the word that the church should be preaching. God's not angry. He's not even in a bad mood. He loves you and has paid the price for you. Receive Him. Receive His love. We shouldn't be proclaiming, "If our country doesn't repent, God's going to judge us. The wrath of God is coming!" It's simply not true. God didn't send the terrorists to kill all those people on 9/11. He didn't send all the hurricanes and tsunamis that have ruined cities and swept so many folks away. That wasn't God.

However, a time is coming when this current age of grace—the church age—will come to an end. The book of Revelation makes it very clear that there will come a time when the Lord says, "All right, that's it." At that time, those who have accepted Him will be received into joy and peace, but those who have rejected Him will suffer the wrath of God. And when God's judgment is poured out as revealed in Revelation, nobody will wonder, *Is this the wrath of God?* They'll all know beyond a shadow of a doubt exactly what's happening. It'll make the devastating hurricanes that hit in 2004 and 2005 look like nothing in comparison. Nobody will be debating or guessing, "Was this the wrath of God?" They'll know it.

But right now, the grace of God is extended toward all people. We should be telling them, "God loves you!" We ought to be saying the same thing the angels sang at the announcement of Christ's arrival on earth. "Glory to God in the highest! Peace on earth from God toward men. God's not angry with you!" Isn't that good news?

An Accurate Representation

Now then we are ambassadors for Christ.

2 Corinthians 5:20

An ambassador doesn't just go over to other nations and proclaim whatever they want. An ambassador must be in touch with their home country so that they can accurately represent them. For instance, every United States ambassador represents the president and the people of the United States of America. They aren't free to make up their own message. Their job is to accurately represent those who have sent them. As believers, we are supposed to be doing the same thing. We're supposed to be representing God.

We are supposed to be having the same ministry Jesus had— and God, in Christ, did not impute man's sins unto them. He went and ate with publicans, harlots, and other sinners the religious system had condemned so much that they wouldn't have anything to do with God anymore. These are the ones Jesus built relationships with and extended love toward. We are His ambassadors. We are supposed to be ministering His message—saying what He's told us to say in His Word.

Most Christians today aren't proclaiming that message. They've adopted a religious system that has been entrenched for hundreds of years. They're saying, "God is angry. If you don't do this and that, He's going to pour out His wrath on you. If you don't do these things, God won't answer your prayer. If you aren't holy, God won't move!" And they're imputing men's sins unto them. Satan is really using that to keep people beaten down and discouraged.

I recently received an email from one of our partners thanking me. This couple had been listening to me for five years, but recently the husband died of a blood clot in the middle of the night. The wife wrote to me, saying, "Because I've been listening to you, I knew what to do." She raised him from the dead. Then he got up, went to the bathroom, and went back to bed. Everything was fine, and she was praising God that she knew what to do according to the Word.

Faith Works by Love

Let's say that you were attending one of my meetings when someone came forward and fell over dead. If I said, "We're going to pray for this person, and I believe God is going to raise them from the dead," you'd probably say, "Go for it, brother!" and eagerly join me up front because you'd want to see it. You'd think, *This is awesome! I'll have a great story to tell everybody else.* You'd be excited until I said, "All right, I want you to pray for the person." Then, all of a sudden, instead of excitement and faith, fear would hit you. Do you know why? That fear wouldn't hit from doubting God's ability but from doubting God's willingness to use His ability through you because you know you aren't worthy.

Most of us believe that God moves in our life only when we're worthy. We've tied His ability to our goodness. The moment you do that, Satan will defeat you because your own heart will condemn you and let you know that you don't deserve it. But that's not the message Jesus brought. He wasn't imputing man's sins unto them. He told us to preach a message that tells people, "The war is over. God isn't mad anymore!"

Now, this doesn't mean that it's all up to God. If it were, then you would receive because God is a good God. He has nothing but good things in store for you. However, you must believe to receive. You don't have to be holy and do everything just right, but you do have to believe. If you feel so unworthy and that you've messed up so badly that God doesn't love you, that's unbelief. That is not the message of the Gospel, and it's the very thing that's keeping your faith from working.

Again, faith works by love (see Gal. 5:6). If you understood how much God loved you—that He carries your picture around in His wallet, that He isn't angry, disappointed, or ashamed of you, and that He's proud of you—your faith would go through the roof. You'd say, "Any God who could love me and overlook all the stupid things I've done is an awesome God. If He'll do that, He'll do anything!"

Gone and Forgotten

Now then we are ambassadors for Christ, as though God did beseech you by us: we pray you in Christ's stead, be ye reconciled to God.

2 Corinthians 5:20

That's my purpose in writing this book. I want to help you become reconciled to God. God has reconciled Himself to you. He has forgiven your sins and taken them away. He's not angry with you. God is now friendly and harmonized with you. Will you reconcile yourself to God? Will you now accept what He has said? This is the message we're supposed to be sharing.

We pray you in Christ's stead, be ye reconciled to God. For he [God the Father] hath made him [Jesus] to be sin for us, who knew no sin; that we might be made the righteousness of God in him [Jesus].

2 Corinthians 5:20,21

The Lord didn't just ignore your sins. He didn't just somehow or another say, "All right, I'm not going to hold their sins against them." He paid for your sins. Your sins are paid for through the Lord Jesus. He not only took your sins away, but then He made you the righteousness of God. Jesus took your sin into Himself and suffered for your sins on the tree. He paid the penalty for your sins and then gave you His righteousness.

You aren't just forgiven. You aren't just an "old sinner" who's been saved by grace. You were an "old sinner," but you were saved by grace and are now the righteousness of God in Christ Jesus. God sees you righteous, holy, and pure. He's not angry with you. It's not a matter of Him just turning the other way and somehow "overlooking" your sins. They've been paid for. They're gone. Your sins have been obliterated.

Your sins have been cast into the sea of forgetfulness. He has forgotten them.

> As far as the east is from the west, so far hath he removed our transgressions from us.
>
> Psalm 103:12

God isn't looking at your sins. He's not dealing with you based on the way you deal with yourself.

CHAPTER 3

Jesus Took It All

Comfort ye, comfort ye my people, saith your God.

Isaiah 40:1

God was actually speaking to John the Baptist in this verse. It was meant to be John's message that he was to proclaim. (Compare Is. 40:3 with John 1:23.) Here's what he was supposed to say:

> Speak ye comfortably to Jerusalem, and cry unto her, that her warfare is accomplished, that her iniquity is pardoned: for she hath received of the LORD's hand double for all her sins.
>
> Isaiah 40:2

Even though the nation of Israel suffered and was led into captivity, no amount of physical suffering—losing their nation, going into captivity, all the terrible things that happened—could pay for all of their sins. You can't pay for spiritual transgressions and sins in the natural.

People who wonder, *How can a loving God ever send anyone to hell?* don't have a revelation of what sin is all about. Sin is such a terrible transgression against God that eternity in a place of torment will still never fully pay for the sins that people have committed. Sin is a terrible thing!

"Woe Is Me!"

I was born again at the age of eight, but the Lord revealed Himself to me in a powerful way at age eighteen. This was the first time I really saw Him, and instantly I had a revelation of His holiness. Even though I was a good person by religious and moral standards, I immediately recognized my relative unholiness and unworthiness. I've never said a word of profanity, never taken a drink of liquor, never smoked a cigarette, and never tasted coffee in all my life. Now, I understand that coffee and alcohol aren't the same thing. There's even scripture to stand on for drinking coffee.

> If they drink any deadly thing, it shall not hurt them.
>
> Mark 16:18

I'm just saying that I've lived a super holy life by man's standards, one that the world might view as holier than most people. Yet once I saw the glory of God, I realized my relative unworthiness and instantly knew in my heart that I deserved to be destroyed.

> When Isaiah saw the Lord in all His splendor and glory, he too fell on his face and cried out:
>
> Woe is me! for I am undone; because I am a man of unclean lips, and I dwell in the midst of a people of unclean lips.
>
> Isaiah 6:5

Every person in the Bible who ever saw the glory of God expected to be destroyed. That's His justice. It's what we deserve. Anyone who says, "I can't believe that a loving God would ever send someone to hell" has never seen imperfect man in the light of God's perfection. They haven't seen the transgressions and total mess of things man has made. Even the so-called "good people" have seriously transgressed against the Lord. There's just no way you can pay for the transgression your sins have made in just this physical life.

"Her Warfare Is Accomplished"

Isaiah 40:2 is a prophetic scripture speaking about the Lord Jesus Christ. It's not talking about how, in the natural, Jerusalem had suffered enough and now God says, "The war is over." This verse is referring to the war God had toward mankind for their sins. It's saying, "When the Messiah comes, He's going to bear your sins. The warfare will be over because your sins will have been paid for. God the Father will have put twice as much wrath upon His Son—the Lord Jesus Christ—as the entire human race was worthy of receiving." Jesus bore our sins and now the warfare is over.

If you continued down through the rest of Isaiah 40, you'll see that the whole chapter is prophetically speaking of Jesus and what He would accomplish when He came. It's saying that John the Baptist was to proclaim to the people that the wrath of God had now been satisfied. The war is over. God's not angry with you anymore. Sin isn't an issue. Jesus has paid for your sins.

Starting with chapter 40 and continuing on through the rest of Isaiah, these are all prophetic scriptures about the Lord Jesus. They contain verses and passages that John the Baptist quoted and made clear that he understood that this was God's instructions to him.

"Marred More Than Any Man"

> Behold, my servant shall deal prudently, he shall be exalted and extolled, and be very high. As many were astonied [astonished] at thee; his visage [face] was so marred more than any man.
>
> Isaiah 52:13,14

Jesus' face was marred more than any person who has ever lived. A man who had cancer all over his face came to one of my meetings in Kansas City. His whole face was a cancer. Another fellow came who had lost his nose. It had been eaten away by cancer. He came forward for prayer with a big towel over his face. Not knowing the situation, I asked him, "Well, what am I praying for?" He took the towel off and I could see right up into his head where his nose used to be. Yet, this scripture says that Jesus was marred more than that.

> His visage [face] was so marred more than any man, and his form more than the sons of men.
>
> Isaiah 52:14

If you study all this out in the original Hebrew language, it means that Jesus didn't even look human. How could this happen?

People said that well-known actor and director Mel Gibson was too graphic in his portrayal of Jesus' beating and crucifixion in the movie *The Passion of the Christ*. However, Mel himself freely admits that he had to tone those scenes down significantly from what the scriptures describe because nobody would have ever viewed them.

According to these scriptures, Jesus' face looked worse than any person who has ever lived. His body was so marred that it didn't even look human. It wasn't recognizable as a human being. It doesn't matter how bad a physical beating someone endures, a whip with small pieces of metal or bone at the tips can't accomplish that.

He Became Sin

Jesus took our sins into His own body on the cross.

Who his own self bare our sins in his own body on the tree.

1 Peter 2:24

He was wounded for our transgressions, he was bruised for our iniquities: the chastisement of our peace was upon him.

Isaiah 53:5

Every sin, sickness, and disease of the entire human race—every deformity, tumor, and perversion—entered into the physical body of the Lord Jesus Christ. That's why His face looked worse than any other person who has ever lived, and His form became so distorted that He didn't even look human. God did this to His Son.

The Passion of the Christ showed only the physical beating. There's no way they could fully depict our Lord's emotional and spiritual suffering too. Who can imagine the agony that came upon Jesus in the Garden of Gethsemane as He thought about becoming sin—the very thing He hated and from which He came to set us free? (See Matt. 26:36–39,42.) He had to become that sin so that we could become the righteousness of God.

In a sense, our religious system today has diminished the atonement of the Lord Jesus Christ. It says, "Even if you're born again and have made Jesus your Lord, God is still mad at you every time you sin. He won't answer your prayer if there's unconfessed (therefore, unforgiven) sin in your life." Basically, we've made Jesus just a part of the solution, but not the total solution. We've said, "Yes, you have to have the atonement of Christ. But you also have to repent, feel terrible over your sin, grovel in the dirt, and do all of these things." People who say these kinds of statements don't understand the totality of the price that Jesus paid for us.

Forsaken by His Father

While hanging on the cross, Jesus said:

My God, my God, why hast thou forsaken me?

Psalm 22:1; Mark 15:34

After putting all of the sin, sickness, disease, and suffering of the entire world upon His Son, Father God turned His back on Him. God forsook His only Son because that was the price that you and I deserved.

By the Spirit of God, I have had just a tiny glimpse of what it's like to be God forsaken. I tell you, that will be hell! Scripture reveals that hell will include physical things like suffering in flames. (See Luke 16:24.) There will be emotional torment too. But the worst part of hell will be the absence of anything good. Everything good—everything God—will be gone. Nothing but darkness, hatred, and strife will remain. Nothing good.

Some of us think we live in a bad world. Sure, there's plenty of corruption in this world, but we don't even have a clue. There is still so much good that is here. There are still people who are going out of their way to make this world a better place to live. As bad as things are, it's nothing like hell. Whether there's any physical suffering or not, total separation from God is hell itself. There's no hope, nothing!

Jesus bore that. He was forsaken by His Father. The Father forsook His own Son so that you and I wouldn't be forsaken. He totally rejected Him so that you and I wouldn't be rejected. All this and people say that Jesus paid for sin only up to a point. "When you sin, God is still upset with you. He turns away from you and won't answer your prayer because of the sin in your life." Wrong!

Some people think I'm making light of sin. The truth is that they're making light of the sacrifice of Christ. Jesus paid such a great and awesome price for us that it forever satisfied the wrath of God. He's not angry with you, regardless of what you've done. Now that's good news.

Nothing Special

Who hath believed our report? and to whom is the arm of the
LORD revealed?

Isaiah 53:1

In other words, this is nearly too good to be true. Who
would believe this? Who can believe that God isn't angry with
you anymore, and He never will be? That all of your sins—past,
present, and even future sins—have been paid for? Not everyone believes this report.

He shall grow up before him as a tender plant, and as a root
out of a dry ground: he hath no form nor comeliness; and
when we shall see him, there is no beauty that we should
desire him.

Isaiah 53:2

Did you know that Jesus wasn't one of these "beautiful"
people? This doesn't necessarily mean that He was ugly, but He
definitely wasn't special. Jesus wasn't one of these people whom
everybody wants to be close to, seen with, and receive attention
from. He was just plain and ordinary. If you had seen Jesus
when He walked here on the earth as a man, you wouldn't have
been impressed. There was simply nothing physically special
about Him.

Sometimes people say, "Oh, I wish I could have been one of
the twelve disciples walking around with Jesus. Wouldn't that
have been awesome?" No, it would've been hard—hard to
believe that this was God! Jesus walked twenty or thirty miles a
day in the hot Judean weather. He didn't have a Holiday Inn to

check into. He didn't take a shower each night before His message. Do you know what? Jesus smelled sometimes. He got dirty. His hair was matted. The Lord didn't carry a suitcase full of clothes to change into. He'd wear the same clothes day after day, and probably week after week as that was normal for people to do living there back then. You had to look past all that. Jesus became like we are.

We portray Him as walking around with a halo over His head, but I guarantee you that people didn't see a halo over His head. He was just as plain and normal as any one of us. Jesus did that for those of us who don't feel special. He felt what you feel. Jesus was looked over, passed over, taken for granted, and unappreciated. Anything you've ever suffered, He suffered those things for you.

By His Stripes

He is despised and rejected of men; a man of sorrows, and acquainted with grief: and we hid as it were our faces from him; he was despised, and we esteemed him not. Surely he hath borne our griefs, and carried our sorrows.

Isaiah 53:3,4

Jesus didn't have any grief of His own to bear. He had never done anything that caused Him misery. The Lord took all of our sorrow, grief, and misery upon Himself.

Yet we did esteem him stricken, smitten of God, and afflicted. But he was wounded for our transgressions, he was bruised for our iniquities: the chastisement of our peace was upon him; and with his stripes we are healed.

Isaiah 53:4,5

People try to limit the application of this verse only to emotional and/or spiritual things. But this verse was quoted in Matthew 8 after Jesus had healed Peter's mother-in-law and many others. (See vv. 14–17.) It says this was done:

> That it might be fulfilled which was spoken by Esaias [Isaiah] the prophet, saying, Himself took our infirmities, and bare our sicknesses.
>
> Matthew 8:17

So the New Testament comments on Isaiah 53:5 show that healing isn't just limited to spiritual and/or emotional things. Jesus suffered so that we could receive healing—spirit, soul, and body—by His stripes.

"The Iniquity of Us All"

> All we like sheep have gone astray; we have turned every one to his own way; and the LORD hath laid on him [Jesus] the iniquity of us all.
>
> Isaiah 53:6

Jesus didn't just suffer in principle for sin. It's not like God gave Him a tiny taste—a sampling—of sin for all mankind. Jesus took all of your iniquity—all the iniquity of the entire world—upon Himself. He literally had the corruption of every sin that has ever been committed on the face of the earth—murder, sexual immorality, and all other ungodly things—enter into His physical flesh. Truly, the iniquity of us all was laid upon Him.

CHAPTER 4

Pleased to Bruise Him

He [Jesus] was oppressed, and he was afflicted, yet he opened not his mouth: he is brought as a lamb to the slaughter, and as a sheep before her shearers is dumb, so he openeth not his mouth. He was taken from prison and from judgment.

Isaiah 53:7,8

This means Jesus never even had a chance to go to prison or have a fair trial. He missed those things.

And who shall declare his generation?

Isaiah 53:8

Jesus didn't have any physical descendants—regardless of what the *Da Vinci Code*¹ book says.

He was cut off out of the land of the living: for the transgression of my people was he stricken. And he made his grave with the wicked, and with the rich in his death; because he had done no violence, neither was any deceit in his mouth. Yet it pleased the LORD to bruise him.

Isaiah 53:8–10

God was pleased to bruise, hurt, and forsake His Son. He made His Son suffer to the point that His face looked worse than anyone else's ever has throughout all of history. He made Him suffer so much that Jesus didn't even look human anymore. God was pleased to do that. It wasn't because He's a masochist or a mean God. It was because He knew that by putting all of our sin upon His Son that He would break Satan's dominion and set the entire human race free.

We Are His Seed

God was pleased to do this because He knew it would totally solve the problem. By His Son's suffering, the sin issue would be forever settled and the war would be over. The wrath of God was fully satisfied by the suffering of His Son. If you think that God is still upset with you, won't answer your prayers, or move because you have some sin in your life, then you don't have a clue what God did to His own Son.

If somehow or another I could transfer your sin to my son and punish him so that I wouldn't be angry with you, I wouldn't do it unless it was sufficient. I wouldn't do it unless it was more than enough. Why in the world would I make my own son suffer if it wasn't going to solve the problem? Yet, by and large, the church has been saying, "Oh yes, Jesus died for our sins. But if you have an unconfessed sin in your life, He won't answer your prayer. God can't use a dirty vessel. He can't fellowship with someone who has sin in their life." Basically, they've just diminished the sacrifice of Jesus.

Yet it pleased the LORD to bruise him; he hath put him to grief:
when thou shalt make his soul an offering for sin, he shall see
his seed.

Isaiah 53:10

This isn't just talking about Jews. It's everyone who places
their faith in the Lord Jesus Christ.

Satisfied

He shall see his seed, he shall prolong his days, and the plea-
sure of the LORD shall prosper in his hand.

Isaiah 53:10

Jesus made His soul an offering for sin because when He
sees the people whom He has set free, that will please Him. The
Lord did all of this because of the benefit it had for us—the body
of Christ.

He shall see of the travail of his soul, and shall be satisfied.

Isaiah 53:11

This scripture says that God the Father was satisfied with
what Jesus paid for your sins. You can't satisfy Him any more.
Your repentance, groveling in the dirt, feeling unworthy and
separated from God, and all these other things cannot add
anything to the way God the Father views you. He is satisfied
with you through Jesus, not through your great goodness. The
only thing you had to contribute was your sin. Sin qualified you.
Then God paid the whole price. The only thing you can do is
either believe and receive or doubt and do without. If you've

made Jesus your Savior, God is satisfied with your payment—not because you've repented and done all these things, but because Jesus has borne all of your sin. That's awesome!

Just As If I'd Never Sinned

He shall see the travail of his soul [Jesus' soul, not yours], and shall be satisfied: by his knowledge shall my righteous servant justify many.

Isaiah 53:11

Justify means "just as if I had never sinned." God saw the travail of Jesus and imputed that justification to me just as if I had suffered and paid for my own sins throughout all eternity. He's satisfied! The payment has been made. Sin has been paid for, and now I'm justified through that just as if I'd never sinned.

God doesn't see me as a sinner. I'm not an "old sinner saved by grace." I am now the righteousness of God (see 2 Cor. 5:21).

My righteous servant [shall] justify many; for he shall bear their iniquities.

Isaiah 53:11

All my sin was placed on Jesus and all His righteousness was given to me. He made me just as if I'd never sinned!

Fruitful

Therefore will I divide him a portion with the great, and he shall divide the spoil with the strong; because he hath poured

out his soul unto death: and he was numbered with the transgressors; and he bare the sin of many, and made intercession
for the transgressors.

Isaiah 53:12

Here's the result of this:

Sing, O barren, thou that didst not bear.

Isaiah 54:1

This isn't talking about just physically being unable to have
children. This is talking about if it seems as though you are spiritually barren; you can't see victory or the blessing of God come
to pass. It just seems like you aren't flowing in the things of God.
Because of what Jesus did—as recorded in Isaiah 52 and 53—
you can sing because you aren't going to be barren anymore.
You're going to:

Break forth into singing, and cry aloud, thou that didst not
travail with child: for more are the children of the desolate
than the children of the married wife, saith the LORD.

Isaiah 54:1

Through the Lord, we can prosper more. We can have more
joy, more victory, more power, and more success than if we
would have had all of these things in the natural. Nobody with
just natural ability and talent can even begin to approach unto
being as fruitful and successful as a person who is doing it
through trusting in the Lord and what He's done for us.

We're Blessed

Enlarge the place of thy tent, and let them stretch forth the curtains of thine habitations: spare not, lengthen thy cords, and strengthen thy stakes; for thou shalt break forth on the right hand and on the left; and thy seed shall inherit the Gentiles, and make the desolate cities to be inhabited.

Isaiah 54:2,3

This is talking about growth, success, and prosperity, not only physically and materially, but emotionally and in every other area too. Through Jesus, you should be expecting nothing but blessings. You ought to be saying, "God loves me. How can anybody be against me?" Instead of saying, "Nothing ever works for me," it ought to be just the opposite. "I'm so blessed, I can't lose for winning!"

You wouldn't be depressed or discouraged if you understood how much God loves you and has forgiven you. It doesn't matter if the doctor has told you that you're going to die. God loves you and you're going to live forever with Him. You've missed hell. Sure, God can heal you and you can live. But if worse comes to worse and you die, you go directly to be with the Lord. We sing, "When we all get to heaven, what a day that'll be!" Then the doctor tells you you're going, and you start crying and falling apart like a two-dollar suitcase. If you just understood that you're forgiven, it would change everything for you.

We win! If we lose, we win. We can't lose for winning. We're blessed. It's impossible to be fearful and depressed thinking about things like that.

God Is for You

This is why Paul was fearless. He had this revelation and knew all of these things. People would tell him, "Quit preaching the Gospel or we'll kill you!" Yet he'd just say, in essence, "This is wonderful!" because he knew that "to me to live is Christ, and to die is gain" (Phil. 1:21).

One time the people told Paul, "Well then, we're going to throw you in jail!" They put him in stocks in the deepest, darkest cell of the prison, but he went to worshiping God. While listening to him sing, the Lord started tapping His foot and caused an earthquake. Suddenly all of the cell doors in the prison opened up, including Paul's, but he didn't leave. (See Acts 16:19–28.) He wasn't just praising God so that he could get out of trouble. He was genuinely worshiping the Lord. It didn't matter to him that his back was beaten and he was locked in some stocks. He didn't care because he knew that God loved him and he was forgiven.

Before then, Paul had been persecuting and killing Christians. But he was so grateful that Jesus had made him just as if he'd never sinned, that he just went to praising. "Now I don't have to worry about what my next sermon is; I can just worship God all night long." The presence of God was so strong in that place that none of the other prisoners tried to escape, and Paul even got the jailer saved. (See vv. 27–34.)

Tell Paul you're going to kill him—he loved it! Persecute him, stick him in the stocks—he thrived! The brand of Christianity most of us have today pales in comparison. We whine if we don't have a brand-new car. Very few Christians have understood what we deserve on our own. Even fewer comprehend what a great price Jesus paid for us.

If you know these things, you have no reason whatsoever to gripe or complain about anything. So what if your spouse left you. I'm not making light over that kind of situation, but God said He'd never leave you nor forsake you (see Heb. 13:5). You ought to be rejoicing over that fact. If nothing else, you could say, "Father, I thank You that in heaven we neither marry nor are given in marriage. Thank You, Jesus!" (see Matt. 22:30). See, it's only temporary.

You don't have a right to be griping or complaining about anything. Almighty God loves you. He's taken your sins. The war is over. You should be saying, "Glory to God in the highest! Peace on earth. Good will toward men." You ought to be planning to break forth on the right and the left with praise and thanksgiving because you're going to prosper, prosper, prosper. Enlarge your tent because God is for you!

CHAPTER 5

Established in Righteousness

O thou afflicted, tossed with tempest, and not comforted, behold, I will lay thy stones with fair colours, and lay thy foundations with sapphires. And I will make thy windows of agates, and thy gates of carbuncles, and all thy borders of pleasant stones. And all thy children shall be taught of the LORD; and great shall be the peace of thy children. In righteousness shalt thou be established.

Isaiah 54:11–14

D o you know why most Christians aren't established? We don't understand that we're righteous. We think we're unrighteous. Since we aren't hearing the true Gospel, we still think that God is imputing sin unto us. That's the reason we aren't established—strong, steady, and secure.

In righteousness shalt thou be established: thou shalt be far from oppression.

Isaiah 54:14

If you are oppressed, do you know why? You don't know that you're righteous. You don't know that your sins are forgiven. We may use that terminology, but with the next breath we say, "God didn't answer my prayer because I have a sin that I just haven't been able to overcome." If you understood righteousness, you'd be far from oppression.

For thou shalt not fear.

Isaiah 54:14

You wouldn't fear if you understood righteousness. Who or what can you fear if God is for you?

And from terror; for it shall not come near thee.

Isaiah 54:14

An Unconditional Covenant

Let's back up to verse 9, which says:

This is as the waters of Noah unto me: for as I have sworn that the waters of Noah should no more go over the earth; so have I sworn that I would not be wroth with thee, nor rebuke thee.

Isaiah 54:9

This covenant that God made with Noah had no qualifications.

I will establish my covenant with you [Noah]; neither shall all flesh be cut off any more by the waters of a flood; neither shall there any more be a flood to destroy the earth.

Genesis 9:11

God didn't say, "If you do this, I'll do that." He didn't stipulate, "If the people never provoke Me again, if they never return to the degree of sinfulness that they were before the flood, then

I'll never destroy the earth again with water." That's not the kind of covenant it was. Noah's covenant was unconditional—no strings attached. It's just a promise that no matter what the world does, God will never destroy the earth with a flood again.

Your Own Conscience

In Isaiah 54, God was saying that this new covenant that Jesus has put into effect is like that covenant with Noah. It's an unconditional, unqualified covenant—in the same way that He swore to never again destroy the earth with a flood, "So have I sworn that I would not be wroth with thee, nor rebuke thee" (v. 9).

For those who enter into this covenant, God is never, ever angry with you. He has never, ever rebuked you. Now, the Lord will show you when you do something wrong. It's not because it isn't paid for. He's already paid for your sins. But God knows that when you yield to sin, you are opening up a door to the devil in your life. If you do that, the Enemy will come in, eat your lunch, and pop the bag! Out of love, the Lord will tell you not to do that—not because He's going to hold it against you or withhold His blessings. He doesn't want Satan to have an inroad into your life.

My three teachings entitled *The Positive Ministry of the Holy Spirit, No More Sin Consciousness,* and *A Good Conscience* all go into much more detail about this than I'm able to here. I encourage you to get them.

God will reveal things to you and say, "Quit doing this," but if you feel guilt, condemnation, and unworthiness, it isn't coming from Him. Religion is what makes you think that God is angry with you, has forsaken you, and put you on the shelf. That's religion—working through your own conscience—condemning you. God is not the author of condemnation.

Covenant of Peace

There is therefore now no condemnation to them which are in Christ Jesus, who walk not after the flesh, but after the Spirit.

Romans 8:1

God isn't angry with you. He has sworn an unconditional covenant. Regardless of what you do, God isn't angry with you. He's never going to rebuke you. All of those times that you've heard people stand up and testify, "I did something wrong and God has just been on my case" aren't true. The Holy Spirit may have shown them that they were wrong, but it was their own conscience that was condemning them and making them feel miserable. At times you may have said, "Well, I sinned against God, and now He's left me," but it's your own conscience that condemned you and cut you off from close fellowship with the Lord.

Think about all of those times you sang David's prayer:

Create in me a clean heart, O God; and renew a right spirit within me. Cast me not away from thy presence; and take not thy holy spirit from me.

Psalm 51:10,11

It's wrong to say that prayer now. David prayed this because he was an Old Testament saint. But as a New Testament believer, God created in you a clean heart the very moment you were born again (see Eph. 4:24). He promised to never leave you nor forsake you (see Matt. 28:20; Heb. 13:5). So every time you feel like God is ticked off at you and has left—you're wrong.

> The mountains shall depart, and the hills be removed; but *my kindness shall not depart from thee, neither shall the covenant of my peace be removed, saith the* LORD that hath mercy on thee.
>
> Isaiah 54:10

The Gospel of Peace

That brings us back to Luke 2:14, "Glory to God in the highest, and on earth peace, good will toward men." God is now at peace with mankind. The war is over. He has made a covenant and signed a treaty. He'll never be angry with us or rebuke us ever again.

> Put on the whole armour of God, that ye may be able to stand against the wiles of the devil....stand therefore, having your...feet shod with the preparation of the *gospel of peace.*
>
> Ephesians 6:11,14,15

Verse 15 says "the gospel of peace." Preaching, "There's war; God is angry and upset; if you don't repent, He won't bless you or move in your life" isn't the Gospel of peace. The reason people aren't responding better is that they haven't heard the true Gospel. They aren't hearing the same message Jesus proclaimed.

Christ had read these scriptures in Isaiah. He wasn't imputing people's sins unto them. He knew what was happening. Jesus understood that He was the Lamb of God who would pay the price and bear all the sins of the entire world. (See John 1:29.) That's why He was able to turn around and extend mercy toward sinners.

Blinded by Religion

We've allowed religion to blind us to the truth that Jesus has paid for all sin—not only for the sins of believers, but also for the sins of the whole world.

> [Jesus] is the propitiation for our sins: and not for ours only, but also for the sins of the whole world.

> 1 John 2:2

Everybody's sins are paid for. Sin isn't the issue. People aren't going to hell because of their sin. They're going to hell because they haven't accepted the payment for their sin. They haven't received the Lord Jesus Christ in their hearts. They don't know Him. They haven't made Jesus their personal Lord and Savior.

You Can't Do Enough

Are you still trying to pay for your sins? Are you doing "penance"? I've actually met a man with grotesque, ugly scars on his hands, knees, and elbows. He had crawled over glass for three miles doing penance. Another guy told me how he had allowed himself to be crucified during the Lent season because he thought it would help atone for his sins. That's an affront against God! It's saying, "Jesus didn't pay it all, and I still have to do something."

Jesus was crucified so that I don't have to be crucified. Now, most of us wouldn't allow ourselves to be crucified, but many of us still feel separated from God. We'll go through a week of being miserable because we feel like we have to do that in order for God to accept us. That's the exact same mindset. It's just a different standard and different set of "penance."

You may think that by going to church, giving extra in the offering, or trying to be good that you're "appeasing" God. You might be appeasing your own conscience, but have you ever truly personally trusted in Jesus? Have you received Him, or are you still trying somehow to barter with God? Are you trusting in the payment Christ made, or in your own good works, hoping that they'll be enough for you to be saved? Be honest with yourself because eternity is forever.

You can't do enough! There's nothing you can offer that will ever supersede what Jesus has done. Jesus plus nothing equals everything. But Jesus plus anything—especially your own effort—equals nothing. Either you have to trust the Lord one hundred percent, or trust yourself, but there cannot be a combination of the two. You either have a Savior who earned you salvation by what He did, or you must earn salvation on your own merit, which cannot be done.

CHAPTER 6

All Judgment

God isn't mad anymore! Sin has been atoned for and He's not imputing man's sins unto them. Remember, when "a Saviour, which is Christ the Lord" was born (Luke 2:11), a multitude of angels praised God singing "Glory to God in the highest, and on earth peace, good will toward men" (v. 14.)

This wasn't talking about peace "among" men, but rather peace from God toward men. Many people haven't understood the difference between the Old Testament and the New. Under the Old Covenant, there was a wrath and punishment from God toward man that was severe. Yet, the Lord doesn't operate that same way under the New Covenant. However, many people have missed this truth and just mix it all together, thinking that God is still dealing with mankind the same way as before. This isn't so.

If you don't understand this truth, it'll negatively affect your relationship with God. How can you draw near to Someone in love if you think He's striking people down with sickness and disease, withdrawing His presence when you sin, and sending the death angel to kill people today? You need to realize that now we have a better covenant based upon better promises (see Heb. 8:6). Under the New Covenant, the relationship between God and man is totally different.

The war is over! God placed the punishment we deserved upon His Son. (See Isa. 53:4–6.) Christ suffered and totally paid the price for our sins. When God the Father saw the travail of Jesus' soul, He was satisfied (see v.11). Now you don't have to suffer separation from God. He's promised never to be angry with you or rebuke you ever again (see Isa. 54:9). These are tremendous truths!

This is a radically different message than the typical church is giving nowadays. Because of that, many people don't understand how much God loves them. Their faith is hindered, and they're having trouble receiving from God. (See Gal. 5:6.)

Spirit to Born-Again Spirit

Most people don't doubt God's ability. What they doubt is His willingness to use His ability on their behalf. Why? They don't feel worthy. The truth is, you aren't worthy in yourself if you just look at your actions. But God doesn't just look at your actions. The punishment for your sin was placed upon Jesus at the cross. Now, He's not only taken your sin away, but He's also given you the righteousness of Christ. In your born-again spirit, you are as righteous, holy, and pure as the Lord Jesus himself.

> Put on the new man [your born-again spirit], which after God is created in righteousness and true holiness.
>
> Ephesians 4:24

God is a Spirit.

God is a Spirit: and they that worship him must worship him in spirit and in truth.

John 4:24

The point is that God looks at you in the spirit realm—Spirit to spirit. He doesn't see you the way you see yourself.

The LORD seeth not as man seeth; for man looketh on the outward appearance, but the LORD looketh on the heart.

1 Samuel 16:7

God isn't looking at your actions, sins, and failures. He's not angry with you the way you're angry with yourself. He's not disappointed with you the way you're disappointed with yourself. God sees you in the spirit, and in the spirit you are a brand-new creation (see 2 Cor. 5:17). God is in love with you. He wants to move in your life, but it takes your cooperation.

You don't have to live holy and earn it, but you do have to believe God. Most of us can't trust that God really is going to move in our lives because we know we don't deserve it. Most likely that's because we've been under a ministry that's been preaching sin-consciousness to us. "If you have sin in your life, God won't answer your prayer. You need to do all of these things first."

The war is over. God isn't imputing our sins unto us. He's not angry with you. God loves you. If you could just receive this good news, your faith would shoot through the roof. You'd start receiving from God, and His supernatural power would operate in your life much, much greater.

Just Thunder?

As Jesus was getting ready to lay down His life for us, He headed to Jerusalem. While there, He prayed:

> Father, glorify thy name. Then came there a voice from heaven, saying, I have both glorified it, and will glorify it again. The people therefore, that stood by, and heard it, said that it thundered: others said, An angel spake to him.
>
> John 12:28,29

These people heard an audible voice from God out of heaven say, "I have glorified Your name and I will glorify it again." Some of them couldn't believe that it was really God speaking. Actually, it's not any different today. People nowadays pray, "O Lord, speak to me. Give me a sign!" If you heard an audible voice from God out of heaven, but your heart was hard, you'd explain it away and think *Oh, that's just thunder,* just as those people did 2,000 years ago. They weren't any different than people today. You need to get to where you hear God in your heart.

God isn't going to speak in a booming voice from out of heaven very often. Even if He did, if your heart was wrong, you'd misinterpret it. You wouldn't believe it. Here was an audible voice from God out of heaven, and these people refused to believe it, saying, "Oh, it's just thunder!"

Jesus answered and said, This voice came not because of me, but for your sakes.

John 12:30

In other words, Jesus didn't need to hear God say this. He was already in communion with and listening to His Father. This came for the unbelievers' sake, and yet most of those unbelievers couldn't even receive it.

"Cross Their Path Carnally"

Now is the judgment of this world: now shall the prince of this world be cast out. And I, if I be lifted up from the earth, will draw all *men* unto me.

John 12:31,32

This is often interpreted as, "If we worship Jesus and preach Him properly, God will draw the people and everybody will come. You'll just instantly have a large church." That's not what this is saying.

I travel around a lot and see many different churches. I don't mean to be critical, but some of the largest churches I've been to have also been some of the worst. They are "seeker-friendly," which means they compromise. They get down to where they have a little twenty-minute message. They have all this lights and flash, but very little Word. Those are the churches that are really growing today—the ones built around entertainment rather than proclaiming the Word. They're making Christianity so easy that a person can attend church an hour a week and feel like they're fulfilling the Scripture's requirements concerning body life. They get their conscience salved, but there's no committal, nothing asked of them.

One time I told the pastor of the 10,000-plus church that I attend, "If you turned this church over to me, I could whittle it down to a thousand in thirty days. If you gave it to me for two months, I could have it down to five hundred. A large portion of these people aren't even baptized in the Holy Spirit." It's simply not true that the churches preaching the best message and lifting Jesus up are having the most people come to them. That's not what I observe happening in the body of Christ. From what I've seen, it's not true that if you'll just preach the right message, God will draw all men to it.

That's the reason I first went on radio. I went to Childress, Texas, and held some meetings there. At the time, I was under the impression that if I just ministered the Word of God, He would draw all men unto me. We started with six people, and by the third or fourth day we wound up with about twenty. After the meetings, I was scheduled to go somewhere else. But the night before I left, God woke me up and said (in my heart), "Andrew, you're assuming that if you're just doing what's right and trusting Me that I would speak to people and bring them to your meeting. If the people were spiritual enough to hear Me say, 'Go hear Andrew Wommack,' I wouldn't need you to minister to them. They aren't listening to the Spirit. They're carnal. Therefore, you need to come across their path in some carnal way." I woke up early that morning and prayed about it. Then I started on the radio the next day.

The Lord said that I had to come across people's paths. So I've been on radio and television ministering God's Word ever since. I send out cards advertising our conferences and citywide meetings, inviting people to come. Most folks just aren't sensitive enough to the Holy Spirit to hear about these meetings and show up on their own. They need us to cross their path in some carnal way.

I've heard stories of believers in countries where they're persecuted for their faith. They just pray, and God leads them where and when to go for the meeting. Every Christian has the capability to hear the Holy Spirit this strongly, but most of us aren't flowing that way. So we use carnal means—like radio, television, computers, and letters—to come across people's paths with the Word.

"When I Am Lifted Up"

Getting back to John 12:32, notice that the word "men" is italicized (in the *King James Version*). This means it wasn't in the original Greek. It's a word the translators supplied to help make the phrase in English be grammatically correct. Since Hebrew and Greek are different languages than English, sometimes translators do this to help make the sentence grammatically correct in English. But at least the translators had enough integrity to use italics to identify these words that aren't truly there in the original language. They are the translators' additions and/or interpretations.

So what then is John 12:32 really saying?

And I [Jesus], if I be lifted up from the earth, will draw all...unto me.

John 12:32

Even though the Lord didn't specify in that particular sentence what "all" would be drawn unto Him, the context makes it clear. Let's consider verse 32 in light of verses 31 and 33.

Now is the judgment of this world: now shall the prince of this world be cast out. And I, if I be lifted up from the earth, will draw all [judgment] unto me. This he said, signifying what death he should die.

John 12:31–33

"Judgment" was the topic of verse 31. In verse 33, we see that Jesus said that verse 32 signified "what death he should die." He wasn't talking about, "If you preach the right message, everyone will come." He was referring to His upcoming death on the cross. In light of this, we see that the topic of verse 31—judgment—carries over into verse 32. Therefore, Jesus was saying, "When I am lifted up upon the cross, I will draw all of God's judgment toward the entire human race to Myself."

"No Condemnation"

All of God's judgment for the entire human race was placed upon Jesus at the cross. God punished Jesus with the punishment we deserved. If God the Father judged His Son with our judgment—punished His Son with our punishment—then it would be double jeopardy for Him to judge you and me today. In a sense, it would be undoing and discounting what His Son—

the Lord Jesus Christ—has done. God has already judged our sin in the flesh of His Son.

> There is therefore now no condemnation to them which are in Christ Jesus, who walk not after the flesh, but after the Spirit. For the law of the Spirit of life in Christ Jesus hath made me free from the law of sin and death. For what the law could not do, in that it was weak through the flesh, God sending his own Son in the likeness of sinful flesh, and for sin, condemned sin in the flesh.
>
> Romans 8:1–3

This word "condemned" means "judged."[1] God the Father judged sin in the flesh of the Lord Jesus Christ.

> That the righteousness of the law might be fulfilled in us, who walk not after the flesh, but after the Spirit.
>
> Romans 8:4

Romans 8:3 says that God judged sin in the flesh of His own Son. He put your sin on His Son and judged Him. In our court system here in the United States, if someone has been judged, sent to prison, suffered, and completed their sentence, you can't retry them. They've already paid the debt. You can't drag them back into court, judge them, and punish them again for something they've already suffered for. That would be what's called "double jeopardy."

Well, Jesus suffered for my sin. He suffered the punishment and separation from the heavenly Father that I deserved.

> My God, my God, why hast thou forsaken me?
>
> Mark 15:34

I am never going to be forsaken by God because Jesus was forsaken for me. I will never be separated from God because Jesus was separated for me. I am never going to be punished by God for my sin because Jesus was punished by God for me. This is so simple, yet most of the body of Christ today is imputing man's sins unto them and saying, "Well, you did this. God would never heal you because you did this. Until you repent of this sin, God can't move in your life." They're making you accountable for your own individual sin. You are having to suffer for your own individual sin.

God Loves You, Stupid!

"But, Andrew, are you saying that there are no consequences to my sin?" *No!* That's *not* what I'm saying. There are plenty of consequences. If you go live in sin, you're stupid! Why? Because God isn't the only person you're dealing with.

God's judgment upon your sin is over. He placed your punishment, rejection, and rebuke upon the Lord Jesus Christ. So God will never punish, reject, or rebuke you. God's punishment upon sin is over. But keep in mind that sin is also an inroad of the devil into your life. The vertical effect of your sin—God's wrath and judgment coming upon you—has been taken care of. However, the horizontal effect of your sin is great.

Know ye not, that to whom ye yield yourselves servants to obey, his servants ye are to whom ye obey; whether of sin unto death, or of obedience unto righteousness?

Romans 6:16

When you yield yourself to sin, you are yielding yourself to the author of that sin. That's why it's absolutely stupid to live in sin—because you're giving the devil an inroad into your life to cause havoc. But God loves you, stupid!

You may be stupid, but God loves you. He's not mad at you, and He certainly isn't punishing you. Does that mean you can just go live in sin? You can sin and God will still love you because He's already placed all of your sin upon Jesus, but it's stupid to give Satan an inroad into your life.

There's Nothing You Can Do

Adultery is one kind of sin that is rampant in the world today. Anyone who would take what I'm sharing and say, "God loves me and my sins have been paid for, so I can go commit adultery" is playing Russian roulette:

- Sexual immorality opens the door for all kinds of sexually transmitted diseases.

- You'll condemn yourself and defile your conscience.

- You'll lose confidence and your own heart will convict you.

- You'll hurt the person you're married to, the one you commit adultery with, your children, and their children—lots of people.

- You'll shame yourself and hurt the kingdom of God.

Whether you've ever committed adultery (or any other sin), God loves you! I'm not advocating living in sin, but I am saying that your sin has been paid for. Jesus drew all judgment unto

Himself and suffered your iniquity, shame, and rejection. He felt whatever you could imagine a person feeling if they commit murder, lie, cheat, steal, and hurt other people. Jesus suffered the shame, embarrassment, and rejection. He suffered the separation from God. He's already done it for us, and for you to bear it is totally unnecessary.

For you to feel that you have to do "penance" and somehow add to what Jesus has already done is actually a disgrace. It's dishonoring Jesus. It's arrogance on our part to think that what Jesus did wasn't enough and that we have to add something to it to make it complete. There's nothing you can do.

> Not by works of righteousness which we have done, but according to his mercy he saved us.
>
> Titus 3:5

We aren't saved by any worth, value, or merits of our own. We have nothing to claim. There's nothing you can do to add to Jesus!

CHAPTER 7

Understand the Gospel

Basically, the way the "Gospel" has been presented today is, "Jesus has paid a price, but it's not a full price. And until you repent and live up to some standard, God can't work in your life. Until you quit dipping, cussing, and chewing, and going with those who do, He can't answer your prayers." We're adding our own goodness, holiness, and works to what Jesus has done. That's the message most of the church is preaching today.

Undoubtedly every last one of us has been exposed to this and have thought that we must do things in order to earn God's favor. You are accepted by God because of what Jesus did—plus zero. All you have to do is receive it by faith. If you're thinking, *Well, I know that Jesus died for me and He did all these things, but I also have to be holy*, that's undoing what Jesus has done.

> If by grace, then is it no more of works: otherwise grace is no more grace. But if it be of works, then is it no more grace: otherwise work is no more work.
>
> Romans 11:6

That's just Old English for "You're either saved by grace or by works, but not by a combination of the two." Either you're saved by the grace of God and all you must do is receive it by faith, or you must be saved by your own goodness and merit (which cannot be done). It's not a combination of the two. It's not Jesus providing the minimum payment and then you adding to it. Jesus paid it all, and it's just a matter of you believing and receiving, or doubting and doing without. That's the way it works.

Yet most of us have fallen under this "works" mentality. Satan is the accuser of the brethren. He can't accuse God, so he focuses his efforts on us. In fact, the devil isn't even trying to tell most of us, "God can't do miracles. God can't set you free, heal you, or bless you." If you believe in God, then—by definition—He can do anything. You aren't doubting that God has the power and can do it. Satan is primarily fighting you by saying, "Sure, God can do things. But what makes you think He would do it for you— you sorry thing!" Then he'll show you that you got mad at someone, that you haven't studied the Word, that you haven't prayed, and so forth. The reason you're missing it is because you tie God's movement in your life to your performance.

As we look at some highlights from the book of Romans, I'd like to recommend both my synopsis of Romans entitled *Grace–The Power of the Gospel* (in audio form as "The Gospel: The Power of God") and my verse-by-verse commentary (which can be accessed free online at our Web site) entitled *Life for Today—Romans Edition* for further study. These go into much more detail than I'm able to here.

Nearly-Too-Good-to-Be-True News

I am not ashamed of the gospel of Christ: for it is the power of God unto salvation to every one that believeth; to the Jew first, and also to the Greek. For therein is the righteousness of God revealed from faith to faith: as it is written, The just shall live by faith.

Romans 1:16,17

The word *Gospel* today is a religious cliché to us. We looked at this earlier, but because so many people don't know what it's talking about we're going to cover it more here.

We use the word *Gospel* to refer to anything to do with church or Christianity. People say, "I'm a minister of the Gospel." Yet, many of these folks don't ever preach anything that's "good news," which as we've seen is what the word *Gospel* means. They're up there saying, "You're a sinner on your way to hell. Repent or else! Turn or burn! I'm preaching the Gospel." That's not the full Gospel. It's true that there is a God and a devil, a heaven and a hell, and if you don't repent you're going to hell. Those things are true, but that's not good news. That's not the Gospel.

There are only two examples in all of Greek literature of this word translated "Gospel" being used outside of the Bible. That's because Gospel means more than just "good news." Remember, it's a superlative that literally means nearly-too-good-to-be-true news. Outside of the Gospel, there isn't anything that's nearly-too-good-to-be-true news. This was a word that existed outside of the Bible before the Bible was written, but it was very seldom used because there wasn't much in life that was nearly-too-good-to-be-true news.

Outside of God and the good things He's done through Jesus, life is bad. Life is a terminal experience. We're all in various stages of dying. If you were to look at life critically—apart from God's goodness, His promises, and the hope of heaven—there are lots of reasons to be upset. If you aren't having a problem right now, just hold on. You'll have one soon. Life is bad. But when Jesus came along and took all of God's wrath and judgment for our sin upon Himself, now that's amazing love!

God Almighty died for us. (See John 10:18; Phil. 2:8.) The whole universe fits within the span of His hand (see Isa. 40:12). Think how big that is. God's hand is bigger than the universe. Yet, He came and lived inside a physical human being. And now He lives in us when we surrender our lives to Him. He bore our sins and died for us. That's nearly-too-good-to-be-true news!

Religious People

Who would die for an ant or a flea? It's so insignificant. That's what we are in comparison with God. He is infinitely greater than we are, yet He loved us enough to die for us. That's nearly-too-good-to-be-true news. He bore our sins. So when Paul used this word *Gospel*, it wasn't a religious cliché. Nobody just passed over this. He was saying, "I'm not ashamed of telling people that God has paid for their sins, that everything has already been done, that God isn't angry anymore."

The religious system of Paul's day just screamed and yelled at this because they were preaching a bad news "Gospel" that wasn't even Gospel. It was just bad news that God is angry and you had to appease Him by doing all of these rituals. You had to measure how many steps you took on a Sabbath, because if you took too many, God would be angry with you.

John the Baptist was raised by the Essenes. They were a group of Jews who lived by the Dead Sea and wrote the Dead Sea Scrolls. In these scrolls, researchers have discovered documents that reveal how legalistic and ritualistic these people were. The Essenes actually taught that it was against the law to have a bowel movement on the Sabbath day. Their reasoning was that it could be considered work and no work was allowed to be done on the Sabbath day. That's the kind of religious system Jesus came into and Paul was addressing. They were people who were so ritualistic and legalistic they thought that if you didn't do all of these laws, God would be angry with you and reject you.

Paul just boldly proclaimed, "I'm not ashamed of telling people that God loves them and that their sins are paid for." We've come full circle today. I've been persecuted for telling people God loves them. I've received much criticism for preaching that Jesus bore their sins and God isn't mad at them anymore. Who was it that persecuted Jesus? Religious people. Who was it that persecuted Paul? Religious people. Can you guess who it is that persecutes the Gospel today? That's right—religious people.

The reason is that they've been taught that God is angry with us and won't move in our lives unless we do certain things. We have a religious pharisaical system in place today, just as in Bible times. But the Gospel is good news!

Salvation Includes Healing

According to Romans 1:16, the Gospel is the power of God unto salvation. *Soteria,* the Greek word translated "salvation" in that verse, doesn't only mean "forgiveness of sins." It also can include healing, deliverance, and prosperity.[1]

> Is any sick among you? let him call for the elders of the church; and let them pray over him, anointing him with oil in the name of the Lord: and the prayer of faith shall save [*sozo*] the sick.
>
> James 5:14,15

The Greek word for *save* here is *sozo* and is used as with *soteria* to denote salvation and deliverance from suffering.[2] Healing is part of salvation. So when the Word says that the Gospel is the power of God unto salvation, this can also mean that the Gospel is the power of God unto your healing. The Gospel is the power of God unto your financial prosperity. The Gospel is the power of God unto your deliverance and emotional stability. If you aren't experiencing peace, joy, and victory; if you aren't healthy in your body; it is very likely that you don't have a full revelation of the Gospel. If you really knew the Gospel—the nearly-too-good-to-be-true news of how much God loves you—you'd realize that your body could be healed.

Many Christians today are promoting all of these natural health products. They're saying that you should go on a vegetarian diet, eat barley grain, and so forth. It's not unusual to watch Christian television or visit a Christian bookstore and see more information available about health, diet, and exercise than the preaching of the Gospel. Now, there's a balance here. But let me say that I don't believe that what you eat and the way you exercise determines 90 percent or more of your health issues. The Bible doesn't teach that.

You might say, "Oh, yes it does!" It talks about these dietary laws, but the only time they are explained is in Colossians.

> Let no man therefore judge you in meat, or in drink...which are a shadow of things to come; but the body is of Christ.
>
> Colossians 2:16,17

Biblical Health

All of these Old Testament dietary laws were shadows and types of New Testament realities that are now fulfilled. For someone to say, "God told me not to eat pork because it's bad for me" is incorrect. It's what the Bible calls a doctrine of the devil.

> Now the Spirit speaketh expressly, that in the latter times some shall depart from the faith, giving heed to seducing spirits, and doctrines of devils...commanding to abstain from meats, which God hath created to be received with thanksgiving of them which believe and know the truth.
>
> 1 Timothy 4:1,3

If someone commands you to abstain from eating meats, Paul says it's a doctrine of the devil. I'm not saying you shouldn't use wisdom, but realize that conventional wisdom about what you should eat changes every ten years or so. I heard a report recently that said a really low-fat diet is detrimental to you. It keeps your brain from working. I've suspected that all along. Your brain has to have a certain amount of fat to work. They change the "standards" all the time.

What does the Bible say about health?

A merry heart doeth good like a medicine: but a broken spirit drieth the bones.

Proverbs 17:22

Honour thy father and thy mother: that thy days may be long upon the land which the LORD thy God giveth thee.

Exodus 20:12

The Bible speaks of operating in honor and joy. If you were to understand how forgiven and loved you are, you'd start rejoicing and praising God. Once you understood the Gospel, your natural realm—your body and soul—would improve. Your immune system would work better if you weren't beaten down feeling unworthy, defiled, and condemned all of the time. You'd have health in the natural realm, whether you received a super-natural healing from Jesus or not.

Perfect Peace

Food and exercise are a part of it, of course, but they're much less than people think. I can't prove this, but I believe that about 20 percent of your health comes from food you eat and from exercise. Most people would say it's 90 percent or higher, but I believe that your joy in the Lord, honoring your parents, and so forth are more important than these natural things. As

Christians, we have—in a sense—become so humanistic. We're ignoring the spiritual roots of things, and trying to find a physical, organic reason for everything.

Take, for instance, the worldly idea about depression: "You're depressed because you don't have certain chemicals." Actually that's not true. The reason depressed people don't have certain chemicals is because they are depressed. If you are battling depression, you can either deal with depression by doing what the Word says—choosing to rejoice in the Lord and encourage yourself in Him—or you can take a pill and have someone dope you up so that you can function. But that's not the right way to do it.

> Thou wilt keep him in perfect peace, whose mind is stayed on thee: because he trusteth in thee.
>
> Isaiah 26:3

"That's true for everyone except those who have had traumatic experiences, were raised in dysfunctional families, or have chemical imbalances." No, that's not what the Bible says. There are no exceptions. If you would keep your mind stayed on the Lord, you would be in perfect peace. If you aren't in perfect peace, your mind isn't stayed on the Lord or it's stayed on religion. If you understood the Gospel, it would produce health, joy, peace, and prosperity. This is awesome!

Intuitive Knowledge

Some Christians say, "Well, people need to know that they're a sinner. They need to know that God is angry with them." In

Romans 1:18–20, Paul basically said, "People already know that they're a sinner. It's an intuitive knowledge. God has revealed Himself from heaven against all sin and unrighteousness of man." You don't need to condemn people. They already have an intuitive knowledge.

Now, they may get into mind games and try to talk themselves out of it. While I was an American soldier in Vietnam, many people told me they were atheists. I remember one guy, a Princeton educated atheist, made me look like an absolute fool because he was just a better talker than I was. But when the bombs started dropping and the bullets began to fly, this guy cried out to the God he said he didn't believe in with all of his heart, saying, "O God, save me!" It's all just a mind game. Let them get into a life-and-death situation and they'll say, "O God, help me!" They know that there's a God. It's just a lie. You don't have to try and convince people of their need for God. Everybody in their heart already knows it. Everybody!

You might say, "But, Andrew, I know someone who doesn't know it." No, you don't. You may know someone who says they don't believe in God, but they know in their heart that there is a God. Don't even argue with their head. Just go straight to their heart and talk to them like they know the truth. You'll find out that people will respond positively.

In the rest of Romans 1, Paul was showing that you don't have to convince people of their sin. They are condemned in their own heart. They know there's right and wrong. Everybody knows that there's only one God, and they are not Him. That's intuitive within every person.

CHAPTER 8

Justified by Faith

In Romans 2, Paul showed that religious people are doubly guilty. They have not only the witness of their conscience, but they also have what they know of the Word of God. For that reason religious people are twice as accountable and doubly guilty before God. So He summed it all up in chapter 3 by saying:

> All have sinned, and come short of the glory of God.
>
> Romans 3:23

Both religious people and nonreligious people know they have a need in their life. Whether they are operating with only an intuitive knowledge of God, or also with the Word of God they've been taught, everyone knows that they need help.

In Romans 4, Paul went back to speaking primarily to religious people. He took the examples of both Abraham and David, two of the greatest Old Testament patriarchs, and showed how they weren't justified—put in right standing with God—because of their holiness. It was the grace of God.

The Lord was very candid in recording Bible characters' sins. David ordered one of his own soldiers killed and then married the man's wife in an effort to cover up his adultery. (See 2 Sam. 11:3–17, 26,27.) Yet, we look at David today and say, "What a great king. What a holy man." The guy committed adultery and murder, yet he was the man after God's own heart (see 1 Sam. 13:14). Of course, I am not condoning adultery and murder, and neither does God. The point is that people who say, "God uses only people who are worthy of being used," and "You need to be holy before God will use you," are wrong.

Faith for Righteousness

God hasn't had anyone qualified working for Him yet. I'm not going to be the first, and neither will you. God has never had anybody who deserved to be used. He was very candid about this.

> If Abraham were justified by works, he hath whereof to glory; but not before God.
>
> Romans 4:2

In other words, if Abraham would have earned all of these things from God because of his greatness, then he might have been able to boast in front of a person, but not before God.

> For what saith the scripture? Abraham believed God, and it was counted unto him for righteousness.
>
> Romans 4:3

That's a quotation from Genesis 15. God had just told Abraham, in essence, "Count the stars in the sky, if you can. So shall your seed be" (v. 5). Abraham just believed God, so his faith "was counted [unto] him for righteousness" (v. 6).

Abraham's wife, Sarah, was his half-sister (see Gen. 20:11,12). According to Leviticus 18:9, this was a sexual abomination to God. If the law had been in effect, Abraham would have been stoned to death. When do you think God decided that marrying a half-sister was wrong? Since He doesn't change, we know it was always wrong. (See Mal. 3:6; Heb. 13:8.) But until the law was given, God was dealing with people in mercy and wasn't imputing their sins unto them. (See Rom. 5:13.) Abraham was living in a sexual abomination to God, and yet he's the only Old Testament person called the friend of God. (See 2 Chron. 20:7; James 2:23.)

He Justifies the Ungodly

God used Abraham because he believed God's promise, not because of his goodness or greatness. Abraham wasn't the sharpest knife in the drawer. He paid tithes to Melchizedek. Melchizedek was a much greater man; he was the priest of the Most High God. According to Hebrews 7:7, the less is blessed by the greater. Since Melchizedek blessed Abraham (See Gen. 14:18–20), he was the greater of the two. Yet God used Abraham instead to start the nation of Israel. He wasn't chosen because he was the best person on earth. Abraham just trusted God and believed His promise. God used him because of faith.

Now to him that worketh is the reward not reckoned of grace, but of debt. But to him that worketh not, but believeth on *him that justifieth the ungodly,* his faith is counted for righteousness.

Romans 4:4,5

God justifies the ungodly. That's the only type of people He can justify. The reason is that He doesn't have anybody else to justify. We're all ungodly! To be *ungodly* is to not be like God. You might be better than I am. You may have lived a better life than I have, but who wants to be the best sinner that ever went to hell? We've all "sinned, and come short of the glory of God" (Rom. 3:23).

We're all ungodly. No one has ever acted consistently perfect like God. So God only justifies ungodly people. If you are unwilling to admit that you're ungodly, you can't be justified. This same principle applies to our relationship with God after we've been born again. The only people God can really relate to and fellowship with are those who are willing to admit that it's not their goodness, worth, or value; but it's coming to Him based on His grace and their faith in the Savior.

If you are trusting your own holiness, that's the very thing that is keeping you from receiving from God. It's the fact that you're saying, "God, give it to me. I deserve it. I've done something that makes me worthy." Those are the only kinds of people whose prayers God can't answer. Why? It's not based on faith in the Savior. You are your own "savior." You are basing God's answer in your life upon your own goodness. That's ungodly.

"The Sacrifices of God"

Even as David also describeth the blessedness of the man, unto whom God imputeth righteousness without works, saying, Blessed are they whose iniquities are forgiven, and whose sins are covered.

Romans 4:6,7

This is a quotation from Psalm 32:1,2. David prophetically saw and spoke of the day of grace when our sins were paid for. David's sins weren't paid for. He had relationship with God by looking forward to the coming payment for his sins, but that payment hadn't yet been made.

The animal sacrifices offered in the Old Testament never really secured forgiveness for anyone's sins. It was impossible for the blood of bulls and goats to take away sins (see Heb. 10:4). They were only a picture—a type and shadow—of what was to come. It was a constant reminder to us that without the shedding of blood—without someone giving their life—we couldn't have relationship with God.

Even though those sacrifices were enforced under the Old Testament, David never offered them for the sins he committed with Bathsheba and Uriah. Notice what Psalm 51, his prayer of repentance over this, says:

For thou desirest not sacrifice; else would I give it: thou delightest not in burnt offering. The sacrifices of God are a broken spirit: a broken and a contrite [repentant] heart, O God, thou wilt not despise.

Psalm 51:16,17

A Slap in the Face

David had a revelation that these blood sacrifices of animals were only types and shadows, and what God really wanted was true repentance from the heart. He didn't offer sacrifices. There's no scriptural account of him doing so. David was looking forward to his sins being forgiven, which is the reason he felt separated from God when he sinned. That's what he was expressing when he said:

> Create in me a clean heart, O God; and renew a right spirit within me. Cast me not away from thy presence; and take not thy holy spirit from me. Restore unto me the joy of thy salvation; and uphold me with thy free spirit.
>
> Psalm 51:10–12

It was appropriate for David to say these things because he wasn't a born-again Christian. He didn't have a new heart. But today, every true believer in Christ has been given a totally new heart. (See 2 Cor. 5:17.) And Jesus promised New Testament believers:

> I will never leave thee, nor forsake thee.
>
> Hebrews 13:5

Since David didn't have this promise, it was okay for him to say these things. But for a New Testament believer to sing "Create in me a clean heart and renew a right spirit within me. Cast me not away from Your presence, Lord. And take not Your Holy Spirit from me" is rank unbelief. It's like slapping Jesus in the face. We have the Lord's promise that He will never leave us nor forsake us. Our sins have already been forgiven. (See 1 John 2:2.) We received a new heart and a righteous spirit the very moment we were born again. (See Eph. 4:24.) Don't ever ask God to give you a new heart after you've already received one. That's unbelief.

For an in-depth look at what happens the instant we're born again, please refer to my teachings entitled *The New You* and *Spirit, Soul & Body*.

Motivated by Love

There's a difference between the way people approached God in the Old Testament and how we approach Him now in the New. They were looking forward to the price that would be paid, and we're looking back upon it. The price has already been fully paid and you are completely forgiven. I'll talk more about forgiveness and confession of sins in a later chapter.

Paul described what David said about the true Gospel:

Blessed are they whose iniquities are forgiven, and whose sins are covered. Blessed is the man to whom the Lord will not [future tense] impute sin.

Romans 4:7,8

This wasn't just "did not" or "does not," but future tense *"will not."* David saw that there was coming such a payment for sin that all sin would be wiped out—past, present, and even future sin would be completely dealt with. "But, Andrew, I can't believe you're saying that a person's sins are forgiven before they're even committed!" That's exactly what David saw. That's exactly what this scripture says. All sin—past, present, and even future sin—has been dealt with and forgiven.

You need to get this understanding. Nothing can come between you and God. You can't blow it. You can't send Him away. He will never leave you nor forsake you. God loves you— and there's nothing you can do about it. Some Christians say, "Man, I would never say that! If you give people that kind of assurance, they'll just go live in sin. What will be their motivation for living holy?" For the most part, the church has been using fear of rejection and fear of punishment to keep people on the straight and narrow. As a whole, the church believes that fear is a greater motivation than love. But that's not true. Love is an infinitely stronger motivation. It's the goodness of God that leads people to repentance (see Rom. 2:4).

No Fear

There is no fear in love; but perfect love casteth out fear: because fear hath torment. He that feareth is not made perfect in love.

1 John 4:18

Whoever fears over their relationship with God hasn't had God's love perfected on the inside of them. Fear has torment, but perfect love casts out fear. Are you serving God because you're afraid that if you don't, He won't answer your prayers, you might lose your salvation, or He will send you to hell? If so, you haven't been made perfect in love. You don't fully understand the Gospel. If you are lacking power for healing, deliverance, joy, and peace, that's the very reason. If there is torment in your relationship with the Lord, that's why. It's the Gospel—the nearly-too-good-to-be-true news of God's love—that releases everything Jesus provided for you. Yet very few people nowadays know the true Gospel.

David knew it. Remember, Paul told in Romans 4:7–8 what David said about the true Gospel. He continued discussing it in the next verse, saying:

> Cometh this blessedness then upon the circumcision [Jews; religious people] only, or upon the uncircumcision [Gentiles; nonreligious people] also? for we say that faith was reckoned to Abraham for righteousness.
>
> Romans 4:9

Receive His Peace

Then Paul discussed how Abraham was reckoned righteous long before he was circumcised and performed this religious duty. Therefore, it was his faith—not his doing of religious duties—that caused God to accept him. Paul used Abraham as an example of faith. Abraham was called the father of many nations before he even had a son. (See vv. 9–22.) That was faith! After Paul talked about all these things, he said:

> Therefore being justified by faith, we have peace with God.
>
> Romans 5:1

It's faith that gives us access to the grace of God (see v. 2). This goes right along with Luke 2:14:

Glory to God in the highest, and on earth peace, good will toward men.

How do you receive this peace? It's through understanding the Gospel and comprehending that God placed your sin upon Jesus. It's not you. You didn't make peace by the fact that you're now going to church, paying your tithes, and that you've promised not to dip or cuss or chew, or go with those who do anymore. "I'll do what's right and then I'll have peace with God." No! Jesus made peace. Christ bore all your sin, and all you can do is receive the gift of salvation. You can't earn it. You can't do anything to make yourself more acceptable to God than what Jesus has made you. The only way you can have peace with God is to be justified by faith.

If you're trying to be justified through your own effort and goodness, that's the reason you have zero peace. If you have to repent, pray through, get born again once more and your sins forgiven every time you sin, then it's all on your shoulders, which is why you have no confidence, stability, or security. "Oh, I know I blow it. But then I run to God and get forgiveness." If this is the way you believe, then you need to place all of the burden of salvation back on Jesus, and not on your ability to recognize and confess every sin.

Many of us do a lot of things wrong that we don't even recognize as sin—but other people do, and God certainly does (see James 4:17). If it were up to you to repent of every single sin and get it "under the blood," you couldn't live that way.

CHAPTER 9

Shall We Sin?

By whom also we have access by faith into this grace wherein we stand, and rejoice in hope of the glory of God.

Romans 5:2

"Access" here is the same word from which we get "admission."[1] When you go to a movie theatre, you pay the admission price and they let you in. This verse is saying that you have access—admission—to the grace of God through faith. Faith is what gains you access to God's grace—not your goodness, works, or performance. God loves you because He is love, not because you are lovely. That's good news!

What shall we say then? Shall we continue in sin, that grace may abound?

Romans 6:1

Paul had been preaching on grace and emphasizing how God loves us independent of our performance. It has nothing to do with our goodness and worth, whether we've done everything right or not. Immediately, this question was raised, "Are you saying that we should continue in sin so that grace may abound?" Paul's answer was:

God forbid.

Romans 6:2

Paul was adamant, declaring, "No, that's not what I'm saying!"

Can We Live in Sin?

Has what you are listening to that is being called "the Gospel" ever made you wonder, *Can I just go live in sin because all my sin has been forgiven?* If you haven't ever had this question come up, then you haven't heard the same Gospel that the apostle Paul preached. He had to address this question many times. Two of them are in Romans 6 (vv. 1–2, 15).

Shall we continue in sin, that grace may abound?

Romans 6:1

Is anyone misunderstanding the message you're hearing? Are they asking the question, "Are you saying that we can just live in sin?" If this logical question isn't coming up, then you aren't hearing the same Gospel that the early New Testament church heard. That's the reason we aren't getting the same results that the early New Testament church had. That's why if most Christians were arrested for their faith, there wouldn't be enough evidence to convict them. There isn't any power or victory in their life. Nobody could even tell they're a Christian.

Do the people around you at work know that you're a believer? Is there anything different about you? If not, then it's because you haven't fully understood the Gospel. You haven't fully comprehended how much God loves you.

God Loves You

Is there something in your life that you've done that you're still ashamed of and haven't admitted to anybody? Are you even trying to hide it from God? The truth is, He already knows all about it. He's already dealt with that sin and forgiven you. Jesus bore it on the cross and suffered that shame for you. He loves you in spite of what you've done.

Regardless of how much you've failed in any area, God loves you. And if you could really understand that and receive it, there would be such a reciprocal love on your part toward Him.

We love him, because he first loved us.

1 John 4:19

If you understood how much God loves you, you'd be a stark raving mad fanatic. "Come on, Andrew. That's not my personality." I'm pretty laid back and quiet myself. Many people don't think I'm anointed when I minister because I don't scream, spit, and yell. But I'm a fanatic. I love God with all my heart. I would follow Him anywhere and do anything He asks because I have a revelation of His love for me. It doesn't matter what your personality type or situation is; if you understood the Gospel, it would release the power of God in your life more than you could ever have dreamed. Instead of being coerced into doing something out of a sense of debt and being fearful that God will be displeased or angry with you if you don't do it, you'd do it out of love. In fact, you'd do it much better, much stronger, and much more out of love than you'll ever do it out of fear.

You need to let people know how much God loves them. They'll serve Him infinitely more out of love than they ever would out of fear. However, it's easier to motivate people—even lost people—out of fear, rejection, and punishment. So, many preachers get up there and say, "If you don't pay your tithe, God's going to judge you. You'll be cursed with a curse!" Unbelievers can relate to that. Those preachers ought to get up there and tell them, "You're free. God loves you. Give as you purpose in your own heart, not grudgingly or of necessity, because God loves a cheerful giver" (2 Cor. 9:7). However, even if people are not under a fear of punishment, that still will not cause them to give freely. It's good not to be motivated by fear, but it's only when preachers motivate people by love that people will in turn love God with all their hearts and give more.

Going Through the Motions

"But the kingdom of God would suffer!" From our human standpoint, the physical things we monitor and keep statistics on may not look as good, but the Lord isn't impressed with those things anyway. It's only those people who give from their heart with the right motivation that God is pleased with anyway. Many people are going through the motions—giving, going to church, reading the Bible, and so on—doing all of the right things, but from the wrong motive. They're trying to earn God's favor and make themselves acceptable to Him. The Lord's not pleased with any of that. That's the wood, hay, and stubble that the Bible says will be torched when we stand before Him. None of these religious works will endure the fire.

> For other foundation can no man lay than that is laid, which is Jesus Christ. Now if any man build upon this foundation gold, silver, precious stones, wood, hay, stubble; every man's work shall be made manifest: for the day shall declare it, because it shall be revealed by fire; and the fire shall try every man's work of what sort it is.
>
> 1 Corinthians 3:11–13

Some big churches have thousands of people attending who aren't really committed to God. Their lack of commitment is causing them to lose out on all the benefits God has for them. There's no real peace, joy, or victory in their lives. They're just going through the motions. That's not pleasing to God.

Many people are just as straight as a gun barrel and twice as empty. They don't have any peace or joy in their lives. Why? They haven't been motivated by the Gospel. They're being motivated out of fear and condemnation. That's not the Gospel.

"Live Soberly, Righteously, and Godly"

If no one asks, "Can I just live in sin because God has forgiven all of my sins?" then they haven't heard the Gospel that Paul preached. The answer to this question is, "Of course not. God forbid! Living in sin is not smart. God loves you so much that all of your sins are forgiven. His judgment isn't coming on your sin. Satan will take advantage of your sin, so you ought to live as holy as you possibly can. But it's not in order to receive God's blessing because you have already received it (see Eph. 1:3). You're just so thankful that you want to live in a way that glorifies God. You don't want to yield yourself to your Enemy who has come to steal, kill, and destroy" (see John 10:10).

I'm glad God raised me up to preach the Gospel because according to religious standards, I've lived a super holy life, which shows that I'm not preaching this so I can indulge my flesh or live in sin. If I were out living in sin, people would immediately say, "Well, no wonder he preaches grace. It frees him to live in sin." But that's not what the Bible says.

> The grace of God that bringeth salvation hath appeared to all men, teaching us that, denying ungodliness and worldly lusts, we should live soberly, righteously, and godly, in this present world.
>
> Titus 2:11,12

If you truly understand the grace of God, you'll live holier accidentally than you ever have on purpose. You'll wind up glorifying and serving God, but you'll do it out of a pure heart. God will be pleased, and He'll inhabit the good works that you do because they aren't trying to earn anything. They're just done out of love. The Lord will be pleased and you'll be satisfied. It'll change your whole life.

This is the Gospel, and we need to be proclaiming it. You need to share the Gospel with your friends, coworkers, and family. It'll release people from religious bondage and set them free.

CHAPTER 10

Eternal Redemption

G od has forever settled the sin issue. People aren't really going to hell because of sin. The sins of the entire world have been paid for.

> [Jesus] is the propitiation [atoning sacrifice] for our sins: and not for ours only, but also for the sins of the whole world.
>
> 1 John 2:2

The sins of lost people have already been paid for. Jesus bore the sins of everyone—not just those He knew would accept Him. People who are rejecting and hating the Lord have already had their sins forgiven.

"Then what's the point in getting saved? Are you saying that everyone is saved?" No, that's not what I'm saying. God has made the payment, but you must receive it. Each individual must appropriate by faith what God has already provided by grace in order for it to take effect in their life.

By Grace Through Faith

By grace are ye saved through faith; and that not of yourselves: it is the gift of God.

Ephesians 2:8

You are saved by grace through faith. You aren't saved by
grace alone. You're saved by grace through faith! Grace is what
God has done for us independent of us. It's completely separate from anything we deserve. By grace, God has already paid
for the sins of the whole world. But you must put faith in God's
grace for it to affect you. Not everybody has responded to
God's grace.

The grace of God that bringeth salvation hath appeared to
all men.

Titus 2:11

God's grace that brings salvation has come to every person.
Even someone like Adolph Hitler, who committed horrendous
atrocities, still had the grace of God extended toward him
according to this verse. Jesus paid for every single one of Hitler's
sins, but as far as we know Adolph never put faith in Christ. He
consulted astrologers and such. There was zero evidence that
he ever truly became born again and every indication that he
went into eternity without God. Since he rejected the payment
for his sin—Jesus—he will answer for those sins. But it's not
because the payment wasn't made. I'm not making light of
Hitler's evil actions, but in Christ, the payment for his sins was
made. Hitler just didn't accept it. So he'll have to pay for his sins

on his own. This is true for all who never accept Jesus as their Lord and Savior.

God paid for the sins of the whole world. Every person's sins have already been atoned for. People aren't going to hell for individual sins. They're going to hell because they rejected the payment for their sins. They're not only rebels and God-haters. Multitudes of religious people go to hell because they thought that by attending church, paying their tithes, reading the Bible, and trying to be good, they could pay for their sins. It is fine to do those things, but they falsely believed that God would accept them because of some worth or value of their own, without receiving Jesus as their Savior. That's not accepting the payment for their sins. They are still trying to make up for their own sins. There will be many people like that in hell.

Savior or Performance?

A Muslim, a Buddhist, a Hindu, and a Christian all stand before God. He asks them, "What makes you worthy to enter heaven?" The Muslim answers first, saying, "I prayed five times a day and gave alms to the poor. I also fought jihad against the infidels, blowing up myself—and many of them—for You. Therefore, I'm guaranteed a place and a harem in heaven." The Buddhist answers next, saying, "I shaved my head, wore a robe, and took an oath of poverty. I denied myself every opportunity I had." The Hindu answers next, saying, "I participated in all of the temple rituals. I honored my ancestors by never eating meat. So, I'm entitled to a better reincarnation." If the Christian were to answer, "I went to church, paid my tithes, read my Bible, fasted, prayed," and so on, then that person wouldn't be any different from the others. Whatever their standards were, all of these people trusted in their own acts of holiness. When asked, "What makes you worthy?" they all pointed to their own performance.

Here's what a Christian who truly understands the Gospel would answer: "It's nothing I did. My faith is in Christ alone, and in His shed blood upon the cross. He's my Savior!" Christianity is the only faith in the world that has a Savior. Every other religious system makes you try to earn God's favor through your own "good works."

It's sad to say, but there are huge amounts of so-called "Christians" trapped in our churches today who are doing the exact same things as Muslims, Buddhists, Hindus, and others in this way—they are trying to be good enough for God to accept them. They think they have to read the Bible, pray, tithe, and so forth, or God won't answer their prayers. While these things are good to do, this isn't true Christianity.

Many other people have been truly born again, but Christ is profiting them nothing in this life. (See Gal. 5:2–4.) Many times the initial born-again experience is presented as a matter of grace. People humble themselves and ask God to save them, while everyone else in the meeting sings, "Just as I am, without one plea." They respond to His grace with faith and receive the Lord. But then they fall into this thinking that says, "I've been saved by grace, but now that I'm a Christian, I need to pray, fast, tithe, study, and attend church in order for God to love me, bless me, use me, and answer my prayers." They may be on their way to heaven, but they have fallen back into the same old legalistic mindset and pattern. This is what Paul wrote about in Galatians 5:2. He said that if you do that, then "Christ shall profit you nothing."

Doubting His Willingness

I am writing this to you in love. I'm not trying to scold you. I'm trying to help you see an area in which Satan has been deceiving and binding so many of us for years. Have you prayed and received Jesus as your Savior? Are you born again, but right now Christ is profiting you nothing? You can't get healed. You don't have joy or peace. You don't have excitement for the kingdom of God, but you're plagued by fear and unbelief instead. If you were arrested for being a Christian, there wouldn't be enough evidence to convict you. Truthfully speaking, there's very little difference between you and the unsaved people at work. In fact, many of the folks you work with would be shocked to find out that you're a Christian. If this describes you, then Christ is profiting you nothing.

It's not because Jesus doesn't have power, it's because we've fallen prey to Satan's lie. We know God is powerful, but we think, *How could He ever use His power on my behalf?* If you feel that way, then you are back under a sin-consciousness, thinking you have to earn God's favor. You know you aren't living as well as you should. Your own heart condemns you. It's not that you doubt God's ability. What you doubt is His willingness to use His ability on your behalf because you feel that He's still holding sin against you.

God placed your sin upon Jesus. Sin is a non-issue with God. He is aware of it and will tell you to quit doing it, but not because He's going to reject you. He's already paid for it. God loves you, and He knows that Satan will destroy you if you choose to live in sin.

> The thief cometh not, but for to steal, and to kill, and to destroy.
>
> John 10:10

The Lord will tell you to quit doing a sin because He knows that the devil will come in, hinder, hurt, and otherwise take advantage of you. God doesn't convict you of sin because He's going to punish or reject you. He's already laid all the punishment and rejection your sin deserved—and then some—upon Jesus. God isn't ignorant of sin in your life, but it doesn't change His attitude toward you. He's paid for your sin—past, present, and even future sins.

If You Miss It, You Miss It

Many people choke on this. They criticize me, saying, "You're a heretic. How dare you say this!" By God's grace, I'm willing to speak the Word in the face of some very dearly held religious traditions.

Some people think that every time you sin, it's a new affront against God and you have to get that sin confessed, under the blood, and forgiven. There are several variations of this. There are those who believe you lose your salvation every time there's an unconfessed sin in your life. If you were to die without getting that sin confessed, you'd go directly to hell. It doesn't matter that you've been born again and walking with the Lord for twenty-plus years. You just lose everything if you have an unconfessed sin in your life. A number of folks teach that if you're driving down the road on your way home from committing adultery (or some other sin), and you have a car wreck and die with that sin unconfessed, you would go straight to hell because you hadn't repented of that sin. That's not what the Scripture teaches.

This is the very reason that most of us aren't experiencing more of God. It's the reason that Christ has become of no effect in our lives. We are limiting what God can do because we've tied it to our worth and value. The truth is that none of us deserve the blessing of God. You and I may not commit adultery, murder, or steal, but we're not perfect.

> Whosoever shall keep the whole law, and yet offend in one
> point, he is guilty of all.
>
> James 2:10

As I said earlier, I've never spoken a word of profanity, taken a drink of liquor, or smoked a cigarette in all my life. But who wants to be the best sinner that ever went to hell? I have sinned and come short of the glory of God (see Rom. 3:23). I've broken God's standard. If you miss a little bit, you miss the whole thing. When someone says, "I don't do these bad things," I always come back and ask, "So, are you perfect? Do you have no sin in your life? Is there nothing wrong?" They answer, "Well, no. I have problems. I've sinned." Well, if you miss it, you miss it.

All Come Short

If God said, "If you can jump up and touch this thirty-foot-high ceiling, then you can be saved," you might be able to jump higher than someone else, but nobody can jump that high. If that were the minimum requirement, we'd all die.

That's how the law works. You can't say to someone else, "I haven't kept them all, but I've done better than you have." There isn't a hell #2 or a hell #3. If you miss it, you miss it!

Remember, we've all sinned and come short of the glory of God (see v. 23). So for someone to say, "I can't believe a person could commit adultery, have a car wreck and die on the way home without confessing that sin, and still go to heaven; there's no way God could accept someone who has just committed adultery!" just isn't true. The same Bible that tells us not to commit adultery also commands us to obey the laws of the land. (See Ex. 20:14; Rom. 13:1–7.) What happens if you drive 56 miles per hour in a 55-mile-per-hour zone? You broke the law. You aren't doing what God told you to do. You may say, "But, Andrew, that's different. There's a huge difference between committing adultery and going one mile per hour over the speed limit."

There may be a difference as far as people and the consequences here in this physical life are concerned, but the same One who said not to commit adultery, also said not to gossip. (See Lev. 19:16.) Gluttony is listed in the same verse as drunkenness. (See Prov. 23:20–21.) The Lord said that if you lust in your heart, it's the same as if you actually did it. (See

Matt. 5:28.). If you hate someone in your heart, it's as if you murdered them. (See 1 John 3:15.) So if you're about to say, "I can't believe a person with sin in their life will be accepted by God," then you might as well give up that idea because all of us have sinned and come short of God's glory.

Entered in Once!

God has dealt with sin.

Christ being come an high priest of good things to come, by a greater and more perfect tabernacle, not made with hands, that is to say, not of this building; neither by the blood of goats and calves, but by his own blood he entered in once into the holy place, having obtained eternal redemption for us.

Hebrews 9:11,12

Jesus entered in once—*once!* This means He doesn't do it over and over again. Every time you sin, the Lord doesn't have to wait until you repent in order to get that sin under the blood. As we just saw, Christ "entered in once into the holy place, having obtained eternal redemption for us" (v. 12).

This wasn't a short-term redemption—only good until the next time you sin (and then you have to repent, get the blood reapplied, and be redeemed again). Christ entered once, and obtained for us an eternal redemption. This pulls the rug right out from under many people. It shakes them to the very core of the foundation of everything they believe.

Backslidden?

Most Christians think that when you come to the Lord, you get your sins forgiven up to that point. Then, every time you sin after you're a Christian, you have to run to the Lord with that sin, repent of it, and confess it. If you don't, then you could die and go to hell with an unconfessed sin, or you're out of fellowship. Religion calls this "backsliding." They say, "You need to repent of that sin and get back into relationship with God."

There's also a milder form of this same wrong doctrine. People will say, "You won't lose your salvation. If you were to die with an unconfessed sin or in a backslidden state, you'd still go to heaven, but you can't enjoy the presence of God. The Lord won't fellowship with a dirty vessel. God can't fill a dirty vessel. He can't answer your prayers if you have any sin in your life." If that were true, then God doesn't have anyone to fellowship with and He's not going to answer anybody's prayer because we all have things wrong with us.

These Are Incompatible

Sin isn't only what you're doing. It's also what you're not doing.

Therefore to him that knoweth to do good, and doeth it not, to him it is sin.

James 4:17

So, sin isn't only violating a command not to do something. It's also not doing the good you know to do. According to this biblical definition of sin, if you know that you're supposed to love somebody, if you know that you're supposed to pray, if you have been convicted by God to love your wife as Christ loves the church or to honor your husband the same way the church is to honor Christ (see Eph. 5:22–26); if you're supposed to do any of these things and you're failing—which if you're breathing, you're failing in some way—then we've all sinned. If it were true that you can't fellowship with God as long as there's sin in your life, nobody could ever fellowship with Him.

We've adopted this lie that every time we sin it's a new affront against God that has to be repented of, confessed, and put under the blood. Because of this mentality and the fact that we know in our heart that we're just blowing it all of the time, we feel unworthy and are void of any real confidence that God truly loves us. We'll say that He loves us, but then we'll turn around and confess, "I know why God hasn't healed me of this cancer. He's letting me suffer. The Lord allowed this car wreck that killed my loved ones. He's the One who sent these tragedies like the terrorist attacks, tsunamis, and hurricanes. God's ticked off!" We say, "God loves us" out of one side of our mouth, and "God is judging us because of our sin" out of the other. These are incompatible.

Jesus obtained for us an eternal redemption.

CHAPTER 11

The Real Deal

The blood of bulls and of goats, and the ashes of an heifer sprinkling the unclean, [can] sanctifieth to the purifying of the flesh.

Hebrews 9:13

The author of this verse was writing to Hebrews—Jewish Christians. They were aware of all the covenants, laws, and rituals involved in the Old Testament. The author was saying, "If the Old Testament sacrifices had any benefit to them, how much greater then is the sacrifice of the Lord Jesus Christ. All those Old Testament sacrifices were pointing toward the sacrifice that Jesus was going to make."

How much more shall the blood of Christ, who through the eternal Spirit offered himself without spot to God, purge your conscience from dead works to serve the living God?

Hebrews 9:14

The problem is that we have a conscience that has been defiled. We haven't purged our conscience with the truth about what Jesus has done with our sins. Satan is dragging up things that you have done, saying, "Sure God exists and He has power, but He won't do it for you, you sorry thing!" We're allowing the devil's condemnation to destroy our faith and confidence in God because we know we don't deserve it. There's good news. It's the Gospel! You don't deserve it, but God isn't giving you what you deserve. You're getting what God deserves. You get to use the name of Jesus, and God isn't angry with you or holding your sins against you. Jesus entered into the holy place one time and obtained for us an eternal redemption. He paid for all of your sins—past, present, and even the ones you haven't committed yet. Your sins have been forgiven.

Eternal Inheritance

"But how can that be?" you may ask. Keep reading.

> For this cause he is the mediator of the new testament, that by means of death, for the redemption of the transgressions that were under the first testament, they which are called might receive the promise of eternal inheritance.

Hebrews 9:15

You don't just have inheritance. You aren't just a family member until the next time you sin—then you lose it, or at least all of the privileges, and God puts you on a list of children who can't receive anything. He doesn't say, "You don't have any of the benefits because you haven't been living right." No! You get an "eternal inheritance."

The very moment you were born again, you became as forgiven as you'll ever be. When you go to be with the Lord in heaven, you aren't going to get more cleansed. In your born-again spirit, you are as perfect and holy as you will ever be. You have a body and a soul that do get defiled by sin. Your conscience gets defiled. Satan comes in and takes advantage of you. Therefore, when you go to be with the Lord, you'll receive a glorified body and soul. But right now—at this very moment—your spirit is as born again as it'll ever be. You are as clean, holy, and pure as Jesus himself is in your born-again spirit. (See 1 John 4:17.)

A New Creature

You may be saying, "But, Andrew, how can that be?" You look in the mirror and see zits, bulges, wrinkles, and gray hairs (what's left of them). You look at this and wonder, *How can I be righteous?* The Word isn't talking about your physical body. Then you search your soulish realm and find thoughts, attitudes, and feelings that you know aren't the way you're supposed to be. Due to this, you think, *I don't understand—how could I be righteous?* It's your spirit—not your soul—that's born again. Your spirit is the part of you that's created in righteousness and true holiness. However, you can't see your spirit in a mirror or feel it with your senses. Your spirit can be perceived only through the Word of God.

Jesus said:

The words that I speak unto you, they are spirit, and they are life.

John 6:63

If you want to know what you're like in your born-again spirit, you have to look in the Word of God. Hold it up like a spiritual mirror. (See James 1:23–25.) When someone asks, "How are you?" most of us answer, "Oh, I have this pain over here and the doctor said this and that." You describe your physical body. Or you'll search your soul and say, "I'm discouraged" or something similar. But neither your body nor your soul is the real you. The real you is that born-again part of you—your spirit. When someone asks you how you are, you ought to hold the Word up, take a look, and say, "I'm blessed with all spiritual blessings (see Eph. 1:3). I'm above only, and not beneath. I'm the head and not the tail (see Deut. 28:13). I am blessed, blessed, blessed!" Most of us don't know ourselves in the spirit. We know ourselves only in the outward man.

> Therefore if any man be in Christ, he is a new creature: old things are passed away; behold, all things are become new.
>
> 2 Corinthians 5:17

Old things pass away and all things become new isn't talking about your body or your soul. Those didn't change the instant you became born again, but your spirit did. In your spirit, you became as righteous, holy, and pure as Jesus is (see Eph. 4:24; 1 John 4:17). You're forgiven and cleansed. You have an eternal redemption and an eternal inheritance (see Heb. 9:12,15). Jesus purges us only one time. He doesn't have to re-purge us.

You may be wondering, *But how could God forgive a sin before I even commit it?* I'm not sure exactly how all this happens, but Jesus died for our sins only one time 2,000 years ago. You'd better hope He can forgive a sin before you committed it because He hasn't died for any of your sins since you committed them. He anticipated. God knows the end from the beginning. He knew the sins of the entire world. Jesus took your sins and paid for them before you ever committed them. That's good news!

Heavenly Patterns

> It was therefore necessary that the patterns of things in the heavens should be purified with these; but the heavenly things themselves with better sacrifices than these.
>
> Hebrews 9:23

The Old Testament tabernacle and temple were full of these symbols of actual things in heaven. There is an actual mercy seat and altar of incense in heaven. God instructed Moses to make sure that everything be made according to the pattern he was given on the mount. (See Ex. 25:40; Heb. 8:5.) He actually saw into heaven and saw the temple there. All these things were pictures of things that exist in the spiritual realm. Each one symbolized something that Jesus was going to do. The veil of the temple represented the physical body of Jesus that separated between the Holy of Holies and the Holy Place. Something happened to this veil when Jesus died.

> The veil of the temple was rent in twain from the top to the bottom.
>
> Matthew 27:51

This symbolized that Jesus' flesh was broken, and that the way to God is now available through Him. All of these Old Testament sacrifices and rituals that they went through over and over were because the people needed to be reminded over and over again. But the real sacrifice that was made for our sins wasn't something that has to be done over and over again. It was done only once.

Jesus died for the sins of the entire world one time. He dealt with all sins of all people for all time. You don't have to go back to the Lord every time you mess up and feel like you have to work your way back into His favor.

Types, Shadows, and Reality

Christ is not entered into the holy places made with hands, which are the figures of the true; but into heaven itself, now to appear in the presence of God for us: nor yet that he should offer himself often, as the high priest entereth into the holy place every year with blood of others; for then must he often have suffered since the foundation of the world.

Hebrews 9:24–26

The high priest went into the Holy of Holies every year on the Day of Atonement and made a sacrifice. There were also daily sacrifices, both morning and evening. Then there were all the other sacrifices people brought every time someone sinned. So the constant flowing of blood and offering of sacrifices in the Old Testament were just pictures. They weren't the real thing. The author was contrasting the priest continually entering in with sacrifices with Jesus entering in only once. If Jesus was doing it the way it was done in the Old Testament, He would have had to offer Himself many, many times. But He didn't. Jesus only offered Himself for our sins once.

Then must he often have suffered since the foundation of the world: but now once in the end of the world hath he appeared to put away sin by the sacrifice of himself. And as it is appointed unto men once to die, but after this the judgment: so Christ was once offered to bear the sins of many; and unto them that look for him shall he appear the second time without sin unto salvation.

Hebrews 9:26–28

This whole passage is contrasting the Old Testament sacrifices with the sacrifice of Christ. In the Old Testament, the same sacrifices were offered over and over again because they couldn't really work. They were only types, shadows, and pictures of the real deal to come. Since Jesus' sacrifice was the real deal, it had to be offered only once. Yet, it dealt with all sins for all people at all times. He entered in once and obtained eternal redemption for us.

"No More Conscience of Sins"

> For the law having a shadow of good things to come, and not the very image of the things, can never with those sacrifices which they offered year by year continually make the comers thereunto perfect. For then would they not have ceased to be offered?
>
> Hebrews 10:1,2

Notice the question mark. If the Old Testament sacrifices could have worked, then they would have quit offering them and here's why.

> Because that the worshippers once purged should have had no more conscience of sins.
>
> Hebrews 10:2

The Old Testament sacrifices couldn't work, so there was a sin consciousness and they offered the same sacrifices over and over again. But the New Testament sacrifice of Jesus did work, and therefore we should have no more sin consciousness. That's radical! This is so different from the way most people think.

A Performance-Based World

Most Christians are sin conscious. It's just ground into us. People don't treat you by grace. They don't say, "Whatever you do, I'm going to love you regardless." There isn't a role model for this. Your employer doesn't hire you by grace and say, "I want you to know that whether you ever show up or not, or do your job or not—regardless of how you act—I'm a grace man. It doesn't matter what you do, you have guaranteed cost of living raises, promotions, Christmas bonuses," and so forth. That's not the way your employer hires you. Like everything else in the world, it's all based on performance. If you don't perform, you get reprimanded, demoted, or fired.

In marriage, we're supposed to love each other unconditionally. However, I've dealt with hundreds of people who have come to me for counseling. They always say, "I'm mad at them for this."

I answer, "Well, you're supposed to forgive them."

"I know, but they did this!"

"Do you know what you're saying? You're giving that person what they deserve instead of loving them unconditionally." Even in marriage we treat people based on performance.

We treat our kids this way too. When they do good, we sing their praises. When they do badly, we punish them. The entire world around us is based on performance.

Yet the Lord made a sacrifice and forgave you. You didn't deserve to be forgiven. God just forgave you because He loves you and He's a good God. That's why we shouldn't have a sin consciousness.

CHAPTER 12

Spirit vs. Flesh

Most of us are just modeling our relationship with God after the way our father, or someone else, has treated us. But God is greater than any person you've ever dealt with. He has forgiven all of your sin, so you should have no more sin consciousness.

Yet the average Christian approaches God, saying, "Oh, Lord, I come before You so humbly today. Please forgive me of my many sins." It's like we feel that if we mention all of our sins—and mention them quickly—then God might not mention them. But if we don't, He'll definitely bring them up. We just have a constant sin consciousness.

Are you someone who has to be sad and cry every time you come before the Lord? Do you feel so ungodly and plead with Him for mercy? Even if you're acting ungodly in the natural realm, you are righteous in His sight if you've been truly born again. If you approach God, saying, "I'm so ungodly and unworthy. How could You love me?" then you're in the flesh. You aren't in the spirit.

Your born-again spirit isn't defiled or ungodly. It's righteous, holy, and pure. You may say, "But, Andrew, you don't know what I've been doing." You don't know what God has done!

Preserved and Protected

Once you believed on Jesus, you were sealed with the Holy Spirit.

In whom ye also trusted, after that ye heard the word of truth, the gospel of your salvation: in whom also after that ye believed, ye were sealed with that holy Spirit of promise.

Ephesians 1:13

Your born-again spirit—or "new man"—was created in righteousness and true holiness.

Put on the new man, which after God is created in righteousness and true holiness.

Ephesians 4:24

Your spirit became as Jesus is, right here in this world.

As he is, so are we in this world.

1 John 4:17

Your spirit became one with the Lord.

He that is joined unto the Lord is one spirit.

1 Corinthians 6:17

Then, all of this goodness was immediately sealed tight with the Holy Spirit.

In whom also after that ye believed, ye were sealed with that holy Spirit of promise.

Ephesians 1:13

When a woman cans food, she sometimes seals the jar with paraffin. This makes an airtight seal that preserves and protects the food within. Airborne impurities are prevented from getting inside and causing the food to rot and spoil. That's how this word "seal" is used in Ephesians 1:13.

When you were born again, your spirit was immediately encased—vacuum packed—by the Holy Spirit for the purpose of preservation. When you fail in any area of your life after being saved, the rottenness, uncleanness, and defilement that come to your body and soul doesn't penetrate your spirit. This Holy Spirit seal keeps the good in and the bad out.

God doesn't look at sin the way people do. To Him, sin isn't only doing something wrong by violating a command. It's also not doing something right that you should have done (see James 4:17). Nobody loves their mate exactly like Christ loved the church. No one is as passionate about ministering to others as they should be. None of us meditates on the things of God as much as we could. So, according to God's definition of sin, everyone constantly falls short.

If you don't understand that the Holy Spirit encased your born-again spirit, your conscience will eventually give you the impression that you've lost the righteousness and true holiness in which your spirit was created. Your conscience, with its knowledge of right and wrong, constantly bears witness to your mind about your thoughts and actions. If you aren't careful, you'll allow the knowledge of your failures to affect you. You'll think, *Well, when I was born again, God gave me a brand-new start, but I've failed since then.* You may confess, try hard, and get back to where you feel like, *Now I'm back on track and everything's fine!* but it won't be long before your conscience shows you something else. If you go up and down like this day after day, year after year, after awhile you'll think, *What's the use?*

Born of God

The truth is, your spirit was sealed when you were born again. Sin, and its effects, cannot enter into your spirit. When you sin, your spirit does not participate. It retains its original holiness and purity—and will for eternity.

> Whosoever is born of God doth not commit sin; for his seed remaineth in him: and he cannot sin, because he is born of God.
>
> 1 John 3:9

This means you are as righteous and holy now—in your spirit—as you will ever be. Yet, many people struggle to understand 1 John 3:9 because its context clearly shows that Christians do sin.

> If we say that we have no sin, we deceive ourselves, and the truth is not in us.
>
> 1 John 1:8

> If we say that we have not sinned, we make him a liar, and his word is not in us.
>
> 1 John 1:10

My little children, these things write I unto you, that ye sin not. And if any man sin, we have an advocate with the Father, Jesus Christ the righteous.

1 John 2:1

These are three instances from the same letter where the writer, the apostle John, talks about sinning. The first two communicate, "If you say you haven't sinned, you're a liar." He adds, "I'm writing to you so that you will not (future tense) sin. But if you do sin..." Then, in 1 John 3:9 he declares, "If you're born of God, you cannot sin." That sounds very contradictory.

Both Scripture and experience reveal that Christians can sin. The context of 1 John 3 shows that verse 9 isn't saying that it's impossible for a born-again believer to do something sinful. Yet, it also clearly says that if you're born of God, you cannot sin. How can this be?

No Big and Little Sins

Some people take 1 John 3:9 to mean you can't "habitually" sin. Several Bible translations now even render it this way. People who think along this line preach, "If you were a drunk before you were saved, you might get drunk once or twice, but if you're truly saved you won't habitually sin. Eventually, you'll see victory in that area, or you weren't truly born again."

In order to embrace this view, you have to categorize sin—which God doesn't. To Him, there are no "big" sins and "little" sins. By His definition, we all habitually sin. We all habitually fail to study God's Word as much as we should. We all habitually fail to love others the way we should. We all habitually fail to be as considerate as we should. We all habitually get into self-centeredness and God has to habitually deal with us about it.

Sometimes, we also pass over things that God calls sin. For instance, the Lord views gluttony the same as drunkenness, adultery, and murder (see Deut. 21:20). Gluttony is a sin that can happen only habitually. You can't become overweight by eating just one large meal. Even if you gorged yourself, it would only make a pound or two of difference. In order to gain an extra fifty to a hundred pounds, you'd have to do it again and again and again. Being overweight is a habitual sin. This isn't to condemn anyone, but to put things in perspective.

If you interpret 1 John 3:9 to mean that you cannot habitually sin if you're truly born of God, then nobody would qualify because we all habitually sin. The only way this can be preached is to say, "Well, you can't habitually do the 'big' sins, but the 'little' ones—yes, you can habitually sin." That's not what this verse is saying.

If you understand spirit, soul, and body, the interpretation of 1 John 3:9 is obvious. Your spirit is the only part of you that's been born of God. Your soul and body have been purchased, but not yet redeemed. So, your spirit cannot sin even though your body and soul can. This means your performance doesn't affect the purity and holiness of your spirit.

This truth is pivotal to your relationship with God. If you tie His acceptance to your performance, you'll always come short. You might do better than certain other people, but your own conscience will condemn you. Eventually, it'll keep you from enjoying God's love and blessings because you know that you've tried and tried, but you still have faults after all these years. When you understand spirit, soul, and body, you know that it was your spirit that changed. Created in righteousness and true holiness, it's been sealed by the Holy Spirit so no sin can penetrate it. The righteousness you were born again with stays uncontaminated. Since God is a Spirit, He always deals with you Spirit to spirit. No matter how you're performing, you can always approach Him in your born-again spirit. That's awesome!

For further study, I recommend my teaching entitled *Who You Are in the Spirit*. It is good to renew your mind to these truths.

Approach God with Confidence

When you sin as a Christian, it affects your physical body, mind, and emotions. Satan has an opportunity against your physical and soulish realms, but your born-again spirit remains sealed. (See Rom. 6:16.) Since your spirit was created in righteousness and true holiness—and sin can't penetrate that Holy Spirit seal—you don't lose your right standing with God. Your spirit is as pure right now as it was the instant you were born again. Your spirit is as righteous at this moment as it will ever be throughout all eternity.

You are the righteousness of God in Christ (see 2 Cor. 5:21). You are righteous in your spirit, and it's sealed. It never fluctuates. God is a Spirit, and He relates to you Spirit to spirit (see John 4:24). He sees you as clean, holy, and pure even though you aren't that way in your physical man. Because you are righteous in your born-again spirit, you can approach God with confidence even though you haven't done everything you should have done in your physical actions. Now that's good news!

CHAPTER 13

Born Again Perfect

Jesus made a covenant with us. He died to put His will into effect, and then rose again to enforce—probate—it. Now, that's a good deal!

> By the which will we are sanctified through the offering of the body of Jesus Christ once for all.
>
> Hebrews 10:10

The Word says that we are sanctified—made holy—through the offering of the Lord "Jesus Christ once for all." This offering wasn't just "once for all people," but "once for all time."

> Every priest standeth *daily* ministering and offering *oftentimes* the same sacrifices, which can never take away sins: but this man [Jesus], after he had offered *one sacrifice for sins for ever,* sat down on the right hand of God.
>
> Hebrews 10:11,12

Notice the contrast between the way it was done in the Old Testament ("daily" and "oftentimes") and the way it's done in the New ("one sacrifice for sins for ever"). Jesus made one sacrifice for your sins forever!

Sanctified

From henceforth expecting till his enemies be made his foot-stool. For by one offering he hath perfected for ever them that are sanctified.

Hebrews 10:13,14

According to verse 10, you were "sanctified through the offering of the body of Jesus Christ once for all." Verse 14 says that if you were sanctified, you've also been perfected forever. These verses aren't talking about your body or your soul. You won't find this perfection there. This is speaking of the part of you that totally changed the instant you were born again—your spirit.

Now your spirit is identical to the Lord Jesus Christ (see 1 Cor. 6:17). It's sinless and sealed (see Eph. 4:24; 1:13). When you sin in your physical body, that sin opens up a door for Satan to come against you with sickness, poverty, and so forth. (See Rom. 6:16.) When you sin with your soul, he'll come in and defile your thinking. Sin makes you spiritually handicapped (hindered or delayed) because of the way it affects your ability to think, but it doesn't penetrate your born-again spirit. Your spirit has been sanctified and perfected forever.

Ye are come unto mount Sion, and unto the city of the living God, the heavenly Jerusalem, and to an innumerable company of angels, to the general assembly and church of the firstborn, which are written in heaven, and to God the Judge of all, and to *the spirits of just men made perfect*.

Hebrews 12:22,23

Your spirit is the part of you that has been made perfect. It would've been wonderful if God had given us a perfect head that knew all things, but this has yet to come. (See 1 Cor. 13:9–12.) In the meantime, we are in the process of renewing our minds to the truth of God's Word. In your spirit, you are sanctified and perfected forever. God has forgiven you of all sin. He's not mad at you because He sees you Spirit to born-again spirit. (See 1 Sam. 16:7; John 4:24.) Now, God is aware that you have a physical body and a soul that does things wrong, but He looks at you in the spirit. You are His workmanship (see Eph. 2:10). If you've accepted Jesus as your Savior, He looks at you and says, "Perfect, holy, pure, and righteous."

The Spirit of Christ

You have all of the benefits and privileges that Jesus has. This is because your spirit was totally changed, not just dusted off or refurbished.

> God hath sent forth the Spirit of his Son into your hearts, crying, Abba, Father.
>
> Galatians 4:6

The Spirit of Christ is in you.

> If any man have not the Spirit of Christ, he is none of his.
>
> Romans 8:9

If you say, "I don't believe that I have the Spirit of Christ," then you need to be born again. If you don't have the Spirit of Christ, then you aren't His. If you are born again, then you have

THE WAR IS OVER

a born-again spirit that is identical to Jesus because it's His spirit on the inside of you. You have His faith, His knowledge, His power, and His victory. Everything that's true of Jesus is true of your born-again spirit, which is sealed by the Holy Spirit so that you'll never lose it.

God deals with you based on who you are in the spirit.

God Possessed

I reckon that the sufferings of this present time are not worthy to be compared with the glory which shall be revealed *in* us.

Romans 8:18

Notice how this didn't say, "The glory which shall be revealed *to* us." Most Christians sing, "When we all get to heaven, what a day that'll be." We think, *Heaven will be so wonderful!* And it will because we'll receive a glorified body that isn't subject to decay, disease, or death. We'll also receive a glorified soul that doesn't struggle with doubt or unbelief anymore, but it knows all things. However, the Word says that the sufferings of this present world are not worthy to be compared with the glory which shall be revealed in us—not *to* us—but *in* us.

When we stand before God, all of a sudden we'll know all things (see 1 Cor. 13:12). In an instant, the Lord will straighten out our theology and we'll understand everything even as we are known. We'll say, "You mean I was forgiven this whole time I went around feeling ungodly and unworthy? You mean I was righteous and holy the entire time I moped around feeling guilty and condemned? I thought You wouldn't do it for me because I wasn't good enough and I hadn't done this and that." You're going to find out that you had the glory of God on the inside of you.

You'll discover that you were as righteous, pure, and holy as Jesus himself. The same power that raised Christ from the dead was resident inside you the whole time. (See Eph. 1:18–20.) Yet, we spend all of our time praying and asking God to send it down, and believing that there were demons stopping our prayer from getting through to God. That's not biblical.

You may say, "But, Andrew, that's what happened to Daniel." No, it's not. First of all, it was God's answer—not Daniel's prayer—that was hindered. (See Dan. 10:11–14.) Second, Daniel didn't have the Lord living on the inside of him like we do today. I don't care what the devil is doing out there—he's not going to block my prayer from getting to God. That's the reason why I bow my head when I pray—He lives within me. I don't need my prayers to get above the ceiling. In fact, I don't need them to get above my nose. He lives right here on the inside of me. I'm God possessed—and so are you if you are born again.

Trust the Spiritual Mirror

That the communication of thy faith may become effectual by the acknowledging of every good thing which is in you in Christ Jesus.

Philemon 1:6

You need to start thinking this way and acknowledging the good things in you in Christ.

The average Christian today believes that God can do anything, but that He has done nothing. They are asking, "Oh God, please heal me. Touch me, and pour out Your love in my life." That's an insult to God. He has already done everything He's going to do to heal you. (See 1 Pet. 2:24.) He has already poured out His love. (See Rom. 5:8.) When you were born again, He put His Son on the inside of you. You have the fruit of the Spirit—love, joy, peace, patience, and more. (See Gal. 5:22–23.) Your spirit is always rejoicing, always healthy, always believing, always full of hope, and always exactly like Jesus is. The only reason you don't benefit from it is that your mind is going more by what it feels in the physical realm than what you see in the Word of God. We trust what we see in a mirror more than we trust what we see in the spiritual mirror. We're basing our life on external things—how we feel and what the situation looks like—rather than on the truth of what God's Word says.

My teachings entitled *Spirit, Soul & Body* and *You've Already Got It!* go into much more detail. These are foundational revelations that God has shown me from His Word. I can't imagine how anyone could truly live a victorious Christian life without understanding these basic truths.

Educate Your Brain

In the spirit, you're changed. You're as clean and pure as you'll ever get. One-third of your salvation is over. When you get to heaven, your spirit isn't going to be dusted off. It won't be given some injection that will bring it up to its full potential. Your spirit doesn't grow and mature. Right now, your born-again spirit is as complete, pure, holy, and mature as it will ever get. Maturity in the Christian life isn't trying to grow your spirit up. It's trying to educate your brain to what you already have in your spirit. You're already perfect!

God loves you not because of what you do, but because of what He did. That's how He can love you even though you've messed up and aren't yet—in the physical and soulish realms—what you're supposed to be. He gave you an eternal redemption and an eternal inheritance. He has sanctified and perfected you forever. Your spirit is perfect. Right now, you can enter into the presence of God. Right now, you have the same rights and privileges that Jesus has because the Spirit of the Lord Jesus Christ lives within you. The only thing hindering us from experiencing all of this is that we don't know what we have.

We've fallen for these thoughts that say, *Every time you sin, God turns His back on you. The Lord is grieved and upset with your sin.* No! Jesus paid for all of your sins. He anticipated everything you've ever done—and will do—and He's already paid for all of them. Now remember, that's not to encourage you to live in sin. If you do, Satan will take advantage of every time you sin. God has already forgiven it, but the devil will walk through that open door into your life and make you pay for it. Sin will take you further than you want to go, cost more than you want to pay, and keep you longer than you want to stay. You don't want to live in sin. We all fail, but the Lord never turns His back on us.

If you think that God turns away from you, won't answer your prayer, doesn't love you, isn't pleased because you haven't been studying the Word as much as you once did, Satan will take that kind of thinking and use it to depress and discourage you. He'll use it to keep you from trusting and believing in the presence and power of God. This is where Satan is beating us. It all centers around sin.

The Devil's Only Inroad

Sin is the only inroad the devil has ever had on us. He's not really telling you, "Oh, God can't do that. He can't do miracles." He's saying, "Sure, God can do it. But you're a sinner. You don't deserve it. He won't do it for you."

You may have more faith in my prayers than you do in your own because you see me on television and hear me on the radio, and you think, *This guy has it all together!* The truth is that if you knew me as well as you know yourself, you wouldn't have any more faith in my prayers than your own. It takes faith for me to believe that God will answer my prayers because I know me! If you feel that way, this is where you're missing it. You're sin conscious and still thinking, *I have to get over these things before the Lord will answer my prayer.*

A woman once asked me to pray with her to get free from smoking. She was ashamed and crying. I said, "You don't go to hell for smoking, even though you smell like you've been there. God isn't mad at you. I don't think it's a good testimony, and it's definitely not good for you. If you don't get free, it makes it hard for you to tell someone else that God can set them free. That's not good." Now, I'm not advocating smoking, and I don't know whether this lady got free or not, but I do know she got free from condemnation.

I received a real education the first time I left the United States and went over to Europe. I was raised in a strict denominational home. We didn't dip, cuss, or chew, or go with those who do. We didn't mow the lawn or do dishes on Sunday. We observed Sunday as the Sabbath, and those things were considered work. We made a real effort to live holy.

My first visit to Austria really played with my denominational mind. There were about two hundred people sitting around tables in this church—and they were serving them beer! Each person received a whole pitcher's worth. They served them all free beer for the entire time I spoke. It was one of the few times nobody minded how long I went. They would have been fine if I had gone on all night long. My little denominational mind was preaching away while all these people were drinking alcohol and praising God.

God Isn't Condemning Us

The Christians drank beer in Austria, but my denomination taught that if you drank or even tasted coffee you went straight to hell. They couldn't believe that a Christian would drink coffee. However, once we crossed the border into Hungary, the Hungarian believers drank both coffee and beer! But they believed that if you smoked a cigarette, you would go directly to hell.

Through this, I began to realize some things. God doesn't treat Americans any different than Austrians or Hungarians. After thinking about it, I realized that some of this is just man's interpretation. Of course, I'm not saying we should drink or smoke.

> All things are lawful unto me, but all things are not expedient [helpful]: all things are lawful for me, but I will not be brought under the power of any.
>
> 1 Corinthians 6:12

These things are damaging to our health, and it's not a good witness. But we've condemned ourselves over them when God isn't condemning us.

CHAPTER 14

Steady and Secure

If our heart condemn us, God is greater than our heart, and knoweth all things.

1 John 3:20

You can feel condemned when God isn't the one condemning you. Many of us say, "God's been on my case beating me up over this sin." No, that's just your religion. The first time I ever skipped a Wednesday night church service was because of my girlfriend. She invited me over to her house. I felt bad about missing church but went to visit her anyway. Once I arrived, there were two other couples already there—dancing! It was bad enough to skip out on church for the first time in my life, but they were *dancing*. I felt so condemned that I thought the Lord was going to kill me.

As a ninth grader, I wasn't driving yet, so I called my older brother and asked him to come and get me. I was at church that night before it was over—on my knees at the altar, begging forgiveness so God wouldn't strike me dead because I'd gone to a place where people were dancing. I was defiled over that for weeks! But God wasn't the one condemning me. It was my own religious thinking.

Many Christians can't even blame the devil for all the condemnation they suffer. All he did was teach them something, and they've been doing such a good job that he's been on vacation ever since. The devil doesn't have to condemn you. You're doing a bang-up job of destroying yourself on your own.

God isn't mad at you. He isn't even in a bad mood. God loves you. He looks at you in the spirit and says, "You're awesome." God sees your potential. He sees His own glory that He's placed on the inside of you.

Foolish Prayers

If it's possible for God to be confused, I believe He would be confused listening to so many of our foolish prayers. "O Lord, take not Your Holy Spirit from me." God's thinking, *Somewhere in the Book I promised never to leave them nor forsake them* (See Heb. 13:5). "O Father, please be with us tonight as we meet." What a ridiculous prayer. In light of that promise—and the one in Matthew 18:20 that says He is with us when we gather together in His name—how could He answer that? "O God, come visit us!" Is the Lord a visitor or a permanent resident? Visitors just come for a brief time and then they're expected to leave. If you're a visitor, you leave after a day or a week, but you don't move in. What a terrible concept. God is with us all the time (see Matt. 28:20). He never leaves us or forsakes us.

We pray foolish prayers because we don't understand that it's already done. In your spirit, you have all of God you can get. You don't need Him to "stretch forth His hand and touch you." He's already put Himself on the inside of you. The same power that raised Christ from the dead already indwells you. (See Rom. 8:11; Eph. 1:19,20.) You don't need more of God. You just need to find out what you have. Then acknowledge the good things that are in you in Christ Jesus, and your faith will start working. (See Phil. 1:6.)

God has already done everything in the death, burial, and resurrection of the Lord Jesus Christ. You already have everything you're looking and praying for. It's already happened. You may be begging Him, "Oh, please forgive me of this sin," when the truth is that He's already forgiven you before you even ask.

"Are you saying that you don't have to repent?" The word *repent* means "to turn and go the other way."[1] Yes, you need to repent—to turn and go the other way—because if you persist in sin, Satan will eat your lunch and pop the bag. You don't need to give the Enemy that kind of an inroad. It's not smart to live in sin. So yes, repent and turn from it, but for what purpose? So that God will accept you? So that you won't go to hell because you lose your salvation every time you sin? If you believe that, how in the world are you ever going to grow and progress?

You don't go through a day without sinning in the sense that you're failing to be everything that you should be. What would it be like if a little child never grew, but had to be born again every day? If children had to get born every day and start over as an infant, there wouldn't be much progression in life.

You don't have to get born again spiritually over and over again, either. There is no such thing as being born again, again. You don't lose your salvation every time you sin. God doesn't fall off His throne because you messed up. He knew it was coming, and has already dealt with it.

"I Still Love You"

My sister is a Christian. She's seen people raised from the dead and loves God with all her heart. When her daughter was a teenager, she was very rebellious. She really knew how to push your hot buttons. One night, my sister was fixing supper in preparation for the dinner guest her husband—a college professor—was bringing home. My niece was in the kitchen smarting off and agitating my sister, but she just kept herself busy getting ready. Finally, my niece said something that pushed her mother over the edge, and my sister slapped her. It took my niece by surprise and knocked her flat on her back in the kitchen!

As soon as she did that, my born-again, Spirit-filled sister dropped what she was doing, ran upstairs, and threw herself across her bed saying, "God, You have to help me. If I start crying, I'm not going to come out of here until the morning. I need to get supper ready and pull things together. Lord, I need a word from You. Help!"

God answered her and said in her heart, "When you were eight years old and asked Me to save you, I knew that you were going to do this. I've already forgiven it. It's okay, I still love you." That allowed her to deal with it and not let sin have dominion over her. She was able to get up and go back down-stairs. It didn't make her say, "Hey, I'm forgiven" and then just beat up her daughter. She went down, asked her daughter's forgiveness, and then got on with the evening. My sister was able to go on because she didn't feel like it was something brand-new that had just offended the Lord and He had to be appeased. He already knew about it and had forgiven her.

It's totally unnecessary for you to agonize over these things you've done. You don't have to feel like you just can't repent of it until you suffer for a while and do penance, saying, "God can't love me. I really blew it this time!" God doesn't look at it that way. He's already paid for your sins. He was satisfied when He saw Jesus suffer for them in your place. Everything you've ever done, Jesus paid for it. God the Father punished, forsook, and actually released anger and rejection toward His Son for your sin. He's not going to make you pay for what His Son has already paid. There's nothing left to pay! You can't add anything to what Jesus has done. There's nothing more you can do. Your wallow-ing in the dirt isn't going to make God love you any more.

God loves you not because of your goodness, but because of Christ's goodness and what He did for you. You need to change the basis of your relationship with God from being your own goodness and performance to relating to God based on faith in what Jesus did for you. When you do that, you'll find that Jesus is the same yesterday, today, and forever (see Heb. 13:8). He never changes. Therefore, your relationship will become steady and secure. You won't have highs and lows. You won't go through the pit and valley feeling like God has forsaken you.

Raised from the Dead

Since the Lord showed me this over thirty-five years ago, I haven't been depressed a single time. Now, I've had depressing things happen and I've been tempted to be depressed, but I know that God loves me. In my spirit, there is love, joy, peace, patience, and all the fruit of the Spirit. (See Gal. 5:22–23.) I've been able to refuse and reject those depressing things and live a happy life. I'm steady and secure.

Even when I was told that my son had died, I was tempted to get into pity, fear, hurt, pain, and grief the same as anybody else would. But I don't like that! I just decided, "I'm not going to grieve over this. I am not going to be upset. Instead of giving in to sorrow, I'm just going to start praising and worshiping God." As soon as I did, faith rose up on the inside. I told my wife, Jamie, "Watch this. This is going to be some awesome miracle!" After our son had been dead for almost five hours, God raised him up. He had turned black, was toe tagged, and lying in the hospital cooler, but now he's alive and well!

I discovered that I'm a new person in Christ, and I'm not going to let what I feel in my flesh dominate me. People who are depressed and discouraged are people who are living in the flesh, looking at the physical realm, and don't know who they are in Christ. If you know who you are in Christ and that your sins have been forgiven, the worst thing that could happen is you die and go directly into the presence of God. If that happens, you'll walk on streets of pure gold and inherit the mansion you'll live in for the rest of eternity. You'll get to personally meet the One who has loved you and died for you. What a great deal!

So you have nothing to be discouraged over. Even if you are given the diagnosis that you're going to die, just kiss the doctor and say, "Awesome! I believe in healing, so I believe God will heal me. But if I'm not healed, it'll be awesome just to sit in His presence 'For to me to live is Christ, and to die is gain'" (Phil. 1:21).

That's not just some preacher stuff. I live that way, and you can too. God is awesome. He's been good to us, and it's only our own religious bondage that is keeping us from appreciating and receiving it.

Don't Be Destroyed

My people are destroyed for lack of knowledge.

Hosea 4:6

Take these truths I'm sharing and meditate on them. God wants to use them in your life in a mighty way.

You don't have to be up and down. If you would get into Jesus and start basing your life on what He has done and not let Satan put you back under the sin that you've been redeemed from, nothing—absolutely nothing—could destroy you. Your faith would go through the roof!

CHAPTER 15

What About 1 John 1:9?

You may be wondering, *If our born-again spirit is sanctified and perfected forever, then why confess our sins?* (See Heb. 10:10,14; 12:23.) *If God is a Spirit and deals with us based on who we are in the spirit* (See John 4:24), *then what about 1 John 1:9?*

> If we confess our sins, he is faithful and just to forgive us our sins, and to cleanse us from all unrighteousness.
>
> 1 John 1:9

Before I answer those questions, let me make some statements.

First John 1:9 is the only scripture in the New Testament that I'm aware of where we are told that if we will confess our sins God will forgive us. There are lots of New Testament scriptures that speak of our sins being forgiven. We've already looked at many of those verses in this book. But this is the only New Testament scripture I know of that makes God's forgiveness of our sins conditional on us confessing our sins. That is a major point.

In Matthew 18:16, Jesus referred to the scriptures—Deuteronomy 17:6 and 19:15—which speak of every truth

THE WAR IS OVER

being established in the mouth of two or three witnesses. This should be the minimum number of scriptures to establish any point of doctrine. And yet, the belief that if we don't confess our sins they won't be forgiven is a major doctrine of the church without other supporting New Testament scriptures.

Jesus' Blood

This concept of repenting and asking forgiveness of our sins before the Lord forgives them came from the Old Testament. Scriptures such as Leviticus 26:40–42; 1 Kings 8:47; 2 Chronicles 6:37–38; 7:14; Nehemiah 1:6; 9:2 and many others, make this a condition of receiving forgiveness. When John the Baptist came preaching in the wilderness, he was still a preacher under the Old Covenant. (See Luke 16:16.) He was announcing the coming of the kingdom of God, but the new birth and all the "in Christ" realities didn't come into being until after the resurrection of Jesus. Therefore, John preached the baptism of repentance *for* the remission of sins. (See Mark 1:4; Luke 3:3.) But Jesus said:

> This is my blood of the new testament, which is shed for many for the remission of sins.
>
> Matthew 26:28

Under the New Covenant, remission of our sins comes through faith in the atoning sacrifice of Jesus' blood. (See Rom. 3:25; Eph. 1:7; Col. 1:14; Heb. 9:22.) It is no longer the turning from our sins that saves us, but the turning to Christ in faith in what He did for us. In Acts 16:30, the Philippian jailer asked

Paul what he needed to do to be saved. Paul didn't ask him what he had done to see what measures he needed to take. It didn't matter what he had done. It was all paid for. (See John 16:8–9; 1 John 2:2.) All of his sins—past, present, and even future ones—were already forgiven. It was simply a matter of whether he would accept what Jesus had already done for him. So, Paul answered:

> Believe on the Lord Jesus Christ, and thou shalt be saved.
>
> Acts 16:31

Faith in Christ

In the New Covenant, we confess our faith in Christ—not our sins—in order to receive the salvation that Jesus has already provided. Romans 10:9,10 clearly expresses this truth, saying:

> If thou shalt confess with thy mouth the Lord Jesus, and shalt believe in thine heart that God hath raised him from the dead, thou shalt be saved. For with the heart man believeth unto righteousness; and with the mouth confession is made unto salvation.

I am not saying that repentance isn't a New Testament doctrine. Many New Testament scriptures promote repentance. (See Acts 20:21; 26:20; Rom. 2:4; 2 Cor. 7:10.) There's even one that links repentance and remission of sins together.

> Repentance and remission of sins should be preached in his name among all nations, beginning at Jerusalem.
>
> Luke 24:47

But there is a difference between preaching repentance and faith towards God (see Acts 20:21; Heb. 6:1) and repentance for the remission of sins, which John the Baptist and the Old Testament prophets preached.

Constantly Cleansed

Let me ask you this question. If you interpret 1 John 1:9 the way it is traditionally interpreted so that we have to confess our sins in order to get them forgiven, then what happens if we don't confess them? Are they not forgiven? And what happens to the Christian who has made Jesus their Lord and yet hasn't confessed every sin? Can you see the problem this presents? For one thing, no one knows all of the sins they commit. Remember, sin is not only the things we do wrong, but it's also our failure to do what we know we should be doing right. (See James 4:17.) Anything not done in faith is sin. (See Rom. 14:23.)

We are constantly falling short of what God wants us to be. That's what fallen humans do; even saved and forgiven humans. But the very context of 1 John 1:9 deals with this problem. First John 1:7 says:

> If we walk in the light, as he is in the light, we have fellowship one with another, and the blood of Jesus Christ his Son cleanseth us from all sin.

Commenting on *katarizo*—the Greek word translated "cleanseth" in this verse—Fritz Rienecker says in his *Linguistic Key to the Greek New Testament*, "The verbs suggest that God does more than forgive; He erases the stain of sin and the present tense shows that it is a continuous process."[1] When we walk in the light of God that we have, the blood of Jesus constantly cleanses us from all these sins of ignorance and omission. What a wonderful truth!

You may say, "But what about the things we do that are wrong and we know they are wrong? Don't we have to ask forgiveness for them?" Yes, we do, but that needs to be clarified too. We've seen that our spirit is the part of us that was born again. (See 2 Cor. 5:17.) In our born-again spirit, there is no sin. (See Eph. 4:24.) We are as righteous, holy, and pure as Jesus. (See 1 John 4:17; 1 Cor. 6:17.) And once we received that pure, born-again spirit, we were sealed with the Holy Spirit so that no impurity reaches our spirit even when we sin. (See Eph. 1:13.) In our spirit realm, we've been sanctified and perfected forever. (See Heb. 10:10,14; 12:23.) Since God is a Spirit and we must worship Him through our born-again spirit (see John 4:24), our relationship and fellowship with Him isn't conditional on our outward actions but rather on our inward heart condition.

Yielding to Satan

However, every known act of sin puts us in a place of submission to Satan.

> Know ye not, that to whom ye yield yourselves servants to obey, his servants ye are to whom ye obey; whether of sin unto death, or of obedience unto righteousness?
>
> Romans 6:16

135

Every time we knowingly yield to sin, we are yielding to Satan—the author of that sin. We place ourselves under his dominion. That doesn't mean we lose our salvation. It just means we have opened a door into our life that allows the devil to do what he wants. Jesus told us what Satan is up to:

The thief cometh not, but for to steal, and to kill, and to destroy.

John 10:10

Satan is the ultimate thief and father of all thievery. So, when we give him place in our lives through knowingly violating God's direction, we can be sure destruction from the devil is on the way. How do we deal with this? That's what 1 John 1:9 addresses.

Shut the Door

First John 1:9 isn't for the purpose of getting our spirit cleansed. We have eternal redemption and eternal inheritance in our born-again spirit. (See Heb. 9:12,15.) But our soul and body aren't sealed, and sin opens them to the power of the devil. How do we reverse that? How do we cancel Satan's legal claim to inflict pain in our lives when we have given him that right? We confess those known sins, and the forgiveness that is already a reality in our born-again spirit comes out into our flesh and drives the Enemy out. The law of the Spirit of life, which is in Christ Jesus, makes us free from the law of sin and death (see Rom. 8:2).

When I realize I've sinned, I repent immediately and ask the Lord's forgiveness. I don't ask in the sense that I think that sin has come between the Lord and me. God is a Spirit. He sees me and deals with me based on who I am in Christ. His love for me doesn't fluctuate based on my performance. I am eternally redeemed (see Heb. 9:12). But my flesh—body and soul—was yielded to Satan through that sin, so therefore I confess it.

The Greek word translated "confess" in 1 John 1:9 is *homologeo*, which literally means, "to say the same thing."[2] When Christians confess their sins, they are simply saying the same thing as God—that that sin was wrong. We are coming back into agreement with the Lord and turning away from Satan. This shuts the door on him and stops his work in our life.

That's why I believe it is necessary for Christians to repent and ask forgiveness for their sins. But it *must* be understood that this only affects their relationship with the devil—not with God.

Perfect in Christ

If we make our relationship or fellowship with the Lord dependent on our confessing every known sin, then there will be some sins that don't get confessed or turned from. That would lead to the broken relationship and fellowship syndrome that religion constantly preaches. This could very well be what has placed you in your current position. You know God exists. You don't doubt that. You know He has the power to move in your life. You don't doubt that either. You just doubt that God is willing to move on your behalf because you don't feel worthy. You believe your sins have separated you from God. (See Is.

59:1–2.) That's not true for the New Testament believer. (See Rom. 8:35–39.)

All sin does for the believer is open a door to the devil. That's bad enough. In fact, that's terrible. So as much as possible, don't sin. But when you do sin, recognize that it didn't separate you from the love of God. He still sees you perfect in Christ, and all your rights and privileges are still there. However, you have made your life miserable by inviting Satan into your affairs. That's why I thank God for 1 John 1:9 and the truths it reveals to us. When you do sin, be quick to repent, confess that sin, and get the forgiveness—which is already resident in your spirit—out into your flesh so the devil can't have his way with you.

CHAPTER 16

God's True Nature

When I first started understanding the grace of God, I had many questions. I saw that Jesus had paid for all of my sins and that God wasn't angry with me anymore. I received a revelation of the truth that God wasn't imputing man's sins unto them and experienced His unconditional love. I knew by experience that God loved me totally independent of my performance. It had nothing to do with who I was and everything to do with who God was. God is a merciful God. I knew that, but as I studied the Word, I ran across a number of things that seemed contrary to this.

Take, for instance, when Ahaziah hurt himself and sent messengers to inquire of Baalzebub whether he would live or die. Elijah intercepted them and said, "Tell the king that he'll surely die because he inquired of Baalzebub instead of God." So the king became mad at Elijah and sent out a captain and fifty soldiers to get him.

Behold, [Elijah] sat on top of an hill. And [the captain] spake unto him, Thou man of God, the king hath said, Come down. And Elijah answered and said to the captain of fifty, If I be a man of God, then let fire come down from heaven, and

139

consume thee and thy fifty. And there came down fire from heaven, and consumed him and his fifty.

2 Kings 1:9,10

So the king sent another captain with his fifty. This captain addressed Elijah and said:

O man of God, thus hath the king said, Come down quickly.

2 Kings 1:11

Elijah answered the same as the first time, and the fire of God fell and consumed all fifty-one men again. (See v. 12.) That's 102 men killed!

"Have Mercy On Me!"

Finally, the third captain the king sent had sense enough to fall on his knees and say, "Have mercy on me and my men! We're just doing what the king commanded us to do!" (See v. 13.)

Then the Lord told Elijah, "Go with them and I'll protect you." (See v. 15.) He spoke to the king, reiterated his previous message, and everything was fine.

Do you know what? Elijah didn't have to kill those 102 men. He didn't have to handle this situation that way. Yet, people nowadays want to imitate these kinds of things. They say, "I'm called to be a prophet—a hellfire and damnation prophet. I'm going to point my finger like Moses did when the earth opened up, swallowed 250 people, and then closed again." (See Num. 16:28–33.) That's the way people want to be today.

There are just some things in the Bible that look contrary to this truth that the war is over. But a closer examination confirms that the Lord is now truly at peace with us.

As Jesus walked along with His disciples, the people of Samaria wouldn't receive Him because they definitely knew He was set on going to Jerusalem. (See Luke 9:51–53.) The Jews in Jerusalem hated the Samaritans because they were a mixed race and had polluted the true worship of God. The Samaritans had already accepted Jesus before. The whole city of Sychar had believed on Him with the woman at the well. (See John 4:1–42.) Yet, when the Samaritans saw the Lord heading for Jerusalem to worship with those hypocritical Jews this time around, they wouldn't even let Him enter into their village. Due to the two most powerful prejudices known to man—racial and religious prejudice—they totally snubbed and rejected Christ.

The Difference

When James and John (known as "the sons of thunder") saw this, they wanted to do what Elijah did. They said, "Lord, do You want us to call fire down out of heaven the way Elijah did?" (see Luke 9:54). They desired to emulate the renowned Old Testament prophet. What could be wrong with that? But Jesus turned around and rebuked them.

Ye know not what manner of spirit ye are of. For the Son of man is not come to destroy men's lives, but to save them.

Luke 9:55,56

Jesus rebuked His disciples for wanting to do the same thing Elijah had done. If Christ had been on the earth in His physical ministry back in the days of Elijah, no doubt He would have rebuked him for calling down fire out of heaven too. That was never God's best. It's not a true representation of Him. Yet, it was appropriate under the Old Covenant.

There is a difference between the way God dealt with mankind under the Old Covenant and the way He deals with us now under the New. If you try to go back and act like an Old Covenant person and relate to God the way Old Covenant people did, then it's no wonder you feel the wrath of God. You're afraid He's going to judge you and separate Himself from you because of the sin in your life. Those kinds of things happened under the Old Testament.

How do we harmonize this? Is God schizophrenic? Is there a God of the Old Testament who changed His mind, got converted in the New Testament, and now He's different? No, God is the same all the time (see Mal. 3:6; Heb. 13:8). So how do we harmonize the judgment we see under the Old Covenant with the mercy we see under the New? We need to understand the true nature of God.

"Until the Law"

Until the law sin was in the world: but sin is not imputed when there is no law.

Romans 5:13

Romans 5:13 is a pivotal scripture that's helped me understand the entire Bible. It says, "until the law." That's during the time of Moses. The law was given nearly 2,500 years after the fall of Adam. Until then, God wasn't imputing man's sins unto them. Until the time that the law was given, man sinned, but God wasn't holding their sins against them. This is a major piece of information!

Basically, our religious system has taught us that God is this holy, stern, austere God who's angry and cannot tolerate sin. It's like He's just leaning over a rail in heaven with a lightning bolt just waiting for someone to get out of line and...*boom!* For many people, this is their impression of God.

Religion has taught us that when Adam and Eve sinned (see Gen. 3:1–7), God instantly cast them out of His presence because He couldn't stand to put up with sinful man. We're told that the wrath of God was instantly vented upon the earth. That's not what Romans 5:13 is saying.

Until the time of Moses, God wasn't holding men's sins against them. God is a merciful God. He didn't instantly start judging man and bringing punishment upon his sin. God was actually operating in mercy toward men for nearly the first 2,500 years of existence. Then the law came and was in effect for the following 1,500 years until the time when Christ came.

Grace and Truth

The law and the prophets were until John [the Baptist]: since that time the kingdom of God is preached, and every man presseth into it.

Luke 16:16

The law was only temporary until Jesus came to end it.

Before faith came, we were kept under the law, shut up unto the faith which should afterwards be revealed. Wherefore the law was our schoolmaster to bring us unto Christ, that we might be justified by faith. But after that faith is come, we are no longer under a schoolmaster. For ye are all the children of God by faith in Christ Jesus.

Galatians 3:23–26

Jesus established grace and truth.

The law was given by Moses, but grace and truth came by Jesus Christ.

John 1:17

In the nearly 6,000 years since creation—2,500 from the Fall to Moses; 1,500 from Moses to Jesus; and 2,000 from Christ until now—mankind was actually under the law with sin being imputed unto them in less than 2,000 of those years. The first 2,500 years, God was dealing in mercy with people before the law. Since the time of Christ, the law has ceased being the way God deals with people. He's not imputing men's sins unto them again.

In spite of this, the church has come along and been proclaiming, "God is holding your sins against you!" So even though we've been out from under the law for 2,000 years, most people don't know it. Most Christians are still living under the law.

"Kicked" Out?

Before the law came, sin was not counted against man. (See Rom. 5:13.) Here's how God dealt with Adam and Eve when they sinned against Him:

> The LORD God said, Behold, the man is become as one of us, to know good and evil: and now, lest he put forth his hand, and take also of the tree of life, and eat, and live for ever: *Therefore* the LORD God sent him forth from the garden of Eden, to till the ground from whence he was taken.
>
> Genesis 3:22,23

Notice the placement of the word "therefore." This means that verse 23 is dependent upon what was said in verse 22. The reason God sent Adam and Eve out of the garden was so they wouldn't eat of the tree of life and would live forever.

These verses don't say that God "kicked" Adam and Eve out of the garden because "He was holy, and a holy God could have no communion or fellowship with unholy man." That's been preached and proclaimed for a long time. "As long as there is any sin, any impurity in our life, a holy God can't have anything to do with us." That's not what these verses say. The Lord made

Adam and Eve leave the garden specifically so they wouldn't eat of the tree of life and live forever.

Still Fellowshipping

Then in the next chapter—after they've left the Garden of Eden—we find God still walking and talking with man. He's still talking with them in an audible voice and fellowshipping with them.

> Cain went out from the presence of the LORD, and dwelt in the land of Nod, east of Eden.
>
> Genesis 4:16

Cain left the presence of God. God didn't take His presence away from man. Man left the presence of God. We walked away from Him. God didn't cast us away from His presence. He didn't quit fellowshipping with man. God was still dealing with mankind in mercy, not imputing their sins unto them until the time of the law.

Why did God send them out of the Garden of Eden? So they wouldn't take of the tree of life, and eat, and live forever in that fallen state. (See Gen. 3:22–23.) It would have been terrible to live forever in a sinful state.

The Benefit of Death

I don't see very many movies, but I do remember one that had a similar theme. This family drank this certain water that made them "live forever." They had already lived over two hundred years and couldn't die. Even when they got shot, they popped right back up again. An evil man had stumbled onto them and their secret. He was tracking them in order to find this water so he could drink it and live forever too. If he had, it would have been impossible to get rid of him. Through this story, the Lord showed me some things.

Because we live in a sinful world, death is actually a blessing. Think about it for a moment. If people couldn't die, then all of the Hitlers, Stalins, Pol Pots,[1] and Idi Amins[2] of the whole human race would still be alive and spewing out their poison. Death ends a lot of things.

What would it be like to live in a fallen world, but not be able to die? You'd live life forever in this corrupted, sinful state. You would live forever in a place where there's just lying, cheating, stealing, and every kind of conceivable evil practice going on everywhere all the time. In light of this, death really is a benefit.

God knew that living forever in sin isn't what He intended for His people. So if you know the Lord, you can look at death as a positive thing in the sense that when it is our time to pass on (see Eccl. 3:2), we get ushered into a different kingdom where everything will be perfect. No more sorrow, crying, or any other kind of suffering. The Lord saw this and didn't want people living forever in a corrupted state. You could say, then, that death is actually a blessing. God didn't want Adam and Eve to disobey Him by eating of the tree of life and having the ability to live forever in corruption and sin. Love—not rejection—motivated God to send Adam and Eve out of the garden.

CHAPTER 17

Acting in Mercy

God didn't quit fellowshipping with Adam and Eve, or their descendants, after He sent them out of the garden. This is evident in Genesis 4.

> In the process of time it came to pass, that Cain brought of the fruit of the ground an offering unto the LORD. And Abel, he also brought of the firstlings of his flock and of the fat thereof. And the LORD had respect unto Abel and to his offering.
>
> Genesis 4:3,4

Most people just read through this and miss the subtle truths embedded within. How did Cain and Abel know that they were supposed to offer sacrifices? Where did they get this knowledge? Was it just intuitive? Did they automatically know these things? Were they born with this knowledge of sacrifice? Although the Scripture doesn't explain, a couple of verses later God spoke to them in an audible voice.

> The LORD said unto Cain, Why art thou wroth?
>
> Genesis 4:6

There is no reason to believe that this was anything other than the same thing that was going on previously in the Garden of Eden. God was walking and talking with them. There was an audible voice. This would be the obvious interpretation due to the context before and after He sent them out of the garden. God was still talking with these people. They were hearing from Him. What was the difference between being in the garden and being out there? God was still walking and talking with them.

How did they know that God approved of Abel's offering and disapproved of Cain's? Scripture doesn't say, but it had to be either some visible or audible manifestation of God, something that showed acceptance and rejection.

Still Walking and Talking

Some people say that the reason Cain's offering was rejected was because it didn't have blood in it. A blood sacrifice is definitely typical of Jesus, but there were other kinds of sacrifices commanded too. What Cain did—offering the first fruits of his crops to the Lord—was commanded nearly 2,500 years later in the law.

> Thou shalt not delay to offer the first of thy ripe fruits, and of thy liquors.
>
> Exodus 22:29

But the Word makes a strong case that the real issue wasn't the substance being sacrificed, but the heart of the person making it.

> By faith Abel offered unto God a more excellent sacrifice
> than Cain.
>
> Hebrews 11:4

The difference was the faith—or lack thereof—in the heart of the one making the offering. I can understand the logic and symbolism of the blood sacrifice argument, but the Word doesn't say that here. Besides, as we just saw, first fruits offerings are later commanded by God as well. (See Ex. 22:29.) These things aside, where did they get this knowledge about bringing these sacrifices? It's obvious to me that God was still walking and talking with man. God was still fellowshipping with man, not imputing their sins unto them. (See Rom. 5:13.) He had respect unto Abel's offering, but not Cain's. There was some visible or audible way that He showed this.

> But unto Cain and to his offering he had not respect. And
> Cain was very wroth, and his countenance fell. *And the* LORD
> *said unto Cain, why art thou wrath.*
>
> Genesis 4:5,6

Again, there's no indication that they had a spirit that was in communion with God or that this was just intuition. From the context, this appears as if God spoke in an audible voice.

Familiarity Breeds Contempt

The LORD said unto Cain, Why art thou wroth? and why is thy countenance fallen? If thou doest well, shalt thou not be accepted? and if thou doest not well, sin lieth at the

door. And unto thee shall be his desire, and thou shalt rule
over him.

Genesis 4:6,7

God was talking to Cain in an audible voice, the same way
He talked to Adam and Eve in the chapter before.

Cain talked with Abel his brother: and it came to pass, when
they were in the field, that Cain rose up against Abel his
brother, and slew him. And the LORD said unto Cain, Where
is Abel thy brother?

Genesis 4:8,9

The average teenager, by the time he or she graduates from
high school, has seen in excess of 250,000 brutal murders on
television and movies. It was totally different back then. They
didn't have television. There had never been a single person
killed on the face of the earth. This was the very first person to
ever murder another person. And while Cain still had the blood
on his hands, God spoke in an audible voice from heaven,
asking, "Where is your brother Abel?"

If you were the first murderer on the face of the earth, you
had just killed your own brother, and you heard an audible
voice from heaven asking, "What have you done?" what do you
think would happen to you? They wouldn't have to worry about
prosecuting you because you'd probably drop dead right there.
You'd be thinking, *This is it!*

For Cain to respond the way he did—lying to the audible
voice of God—speaks volumes. Basically, Cain said, "I don't
know where he is. Am I my brother's keeper?" (see v. 9). It's

obvious that Cain was used to the voice of God. He was accustomed to God talking to him. As the saying goes, familiarity breeds contempt, and no doubt that was the case for Cain.

All this proves that God was still walking and talking with man. This whole concept that when Adam and Eve sinned there was immediate rejection by God simply isn't the truth. God was extending mercy toward man. He was still dealing with them in love and compassion. God was still walking and talking with them.

A Covenant with God

> Cain went out from the presence of the LORD, and dwelt in the land of Nod, on the east of Eden.
>
> Genesis 4:16

Cain was the one who left God's presence, not vice versa. He couldn't stand to be in the presence of a holy God because his own conscience was condemning him. So he left the presence of God. You can't leave something you don't have. The presence of God had to be with him. God was walking with man, still being merciful to them and not imputing their sins unto them during those first 2,500 years.

Abraham married his half-sister. (See Gen. 20:12.) This was an abomination in the sight of the Lord. (See Lev. 18:9,11.) Under the law, the Israelites were commanded to kill people who did this. (See v. 29.). Abraham was living in a sexual abomination to God. When do you think he decided it was wrong to marry a half-sister? Although this wasn't communicated until the law came, God is the same yesterday, today, and forever (see Heb. 13:8). He never intended for these kinds of things to happen. Abraham married his half-sister, but instead of God punishing him, He dealt with him in mercy and made him His friend. (See 2 Chron. 20:7; Isa. 41:8; James 2:23.)

Then Abraham lied twice. (See Gen. 12:10–20; 20:1–18.) On two separate occasions, Abraham was going to let someone else commit adultery with his wife in order to save his own neck. Any way you slice it, that's wrong. It's not integrity. If a wealthy, powerful man in another country took a liking to my wife and I thought, *He's going to kill me to get to her,* and I told him, "I've never seen this woman in my life; help yourself," there'd be a scandal! I'd be criticized—and rightly so—if I did that. It was wrong on Abraham's part, yet God blessed him and rebuked the king as if he were the one who was wrong. Why? The reason is that Abraham had a covenant with God, and the king didn't.

God deals with people based on covenants, not who's right and who's wrong. He protected Abraham.

"Show No Mercy"

Then Abraham's grandchildren came along. Jacob married two sisters—Leah and Rachel—while they were both alive. That's an abomination in God's sight too. (See Lev. 18:18.) Under the law, people were supposed to be put to death for that. (See v. 29.) Yet he wrestled with God and prevailed. So the Lord changed his name from Jacob to Israel. (See Gen. 32:24–28.)

The children of Israel were named after him. On and on we could go in the Scriptures with examples of the Lord dealing with people in mercy.

If the law would have been in effect, they would have been under the wrath and punishment of God. But prior to the law, God dealt with people in mercy, not imputing their sins unto them (see Rom. 5:13).

When Cain killed his brother, he lied to God about it and tried to cover it up. There wasn't any repentance on his part. Cain was sorry he'd been caught, but he wasn't sorry he had killed his brother. Cain told God, "I'm afraid people will hear about this and try to kill me." So God put a mark on his forehead and said, "If anyone touches Cain, I'll avenge him seven-fold" (see Gen. 4:15). God protected the first murderer on the face of the earth. God didn't approve of what Cain had done, but instead of judging and killing him, God extended mercy.

Compare this to the first man who broke the law. (See Num. 15:32–36.) He went out on the Sabbath day to pick up sticks. The first person who ever broke the commandment of Moses was a man who was just gathering sticks so that he could fix a fire and cook some food. They shut him up until they could hear what God wanted to do. The Lord appeared in a visible form of a cloud, and an audible voice spoke, saying, "He must be put to death by stoning" (see v. 35). In other words, "Show no mercy."

Under the law, the first person to violate the law was killed for picking up sticks to make a fire. The first person who transgressed after the fall of Adam and Eve killed his brother and the Lord extended mercy toward him. Can you see the difference between God's dealings with people during the law, and before and after? The law wasn't truly God's heart.

Cutting Out the Sin Cancer

If God really was as angry with people as we have presented Him to be, and as the law sometimes makes Him look, then God would have just started judging people. He would have let Cain have it and had him put to death too. But instead, we see mercy extended toward people.

"But what about the flood and the destruction of Sodom and Gomorrah? Those happened before the law." In these two cases, God acted in judgment toward a certain segment of mankind in order to show mercy toward the human race as a whole. It's like a person who has an infection in their arm or leg. This infection is starting to spread, and it can't be stopped. So the only thing to do is lop off the leg or cut off the arm. It's a terrible judgment on that individual member, but it preserves the life of the body as a whole. Sometimes drastic measures are necessary for the overall good.

During the days of Noah, God destroyed the earth—except for eight people and a bunch of animals—with a flood. (See Gen. 6,7.) During the time of Lot, He destroyed the cities of Sodom and Gomorrah. (See Gen. 19.) It was like there was a cancer in the earth. These people couldn't be purged and cleansed of their sin because they couldn't be born again (Jesus hadn't come, died, and resurrected yet). They were very demonic. I could go into a lot of detail on this, but the Bible says that we are just now beginning to come back to a time that even approaches how bad it was in those days.

> As it was in the days of Noe [Noah], so shall it be also in the days of the Son of man... Likewise also as it was in the days of Lot... Even thus shall it be in the day when the Son of man is revealed.
>
> Luke 17:26, 28, 30

We are just now beginning to come back to a time that even approaches how bad it was in those days. So when you look at all the corruption and sin of today, it still isn't as bad now as it was back in the days of Sodom and Gomorrah. The sin cancer was so bad in the earth that if God had not destroyed those people, there wouldn't have been a virgin left for Him to fulfill His promise through. That's how corrupt the earth was becoming. Acting in mercy toward mankind as a whole, God cut out the "cancer" so that the corruption couldn't escalate and spread to a point of defiling the entire human race.

"I'm Going to Spank You"

As a whole, God wasn't holding men's sins against them. (See Rom. 5:13.) He was being merciful to people. So we find mercy and grace extended toward people and God using people who were doing things that later proved to be totally against His will. Yet, He used and blessed these people.

Then the law came and began holding people's sins against them. It served as a "schoolmaster to bring us unto Christ" (Gal. 3:24). The law shut us up "unto the faith which should afterwards be revealed" (v. 23). But now that Christ has come, we're no longer under this schoolmaster (see v. 25). The reason is that the law was only temporary.

When a child is only one year old, you have to tell them right and wrong and help them start establishing patterns of choosing good things and rejecting bad. Yet, a one-year-old doesn't have the ability to comprehend everything. You can't just sit down and reason with a one-year-old and explain things to them. But you still must get them to where they obey you, not because they understand what's going on, but basically because they fear you (in the right way, not because of child abuse).

I'm sure you've heard an adult say to a young child, "If you do that again, I'm going to spank you." You can't just sit down with them and say, "Now look, if you go over there and take that toy from your sibling, then you're responding to the devil. Satan is a taker, not a giver. The Lord says, 'It's more blessed to give than to receive.' So you're yielding yourself to the devil and establishing a bad life pattern. You'll never have friends because you'll be a selfish person. People don't like selfish people. You'll never be able to hold a job because if you get one, all it'll be is about yourself. Your marriage will fail if you continue in this selfishness." If you try to explain that to a one-year-old, they'll just look at you. They can't comprehend all that.

But you can say, "If you take that toy again, I'm going to have to spank you." They may not even know there is a God or devil, heaven or hell, but when they feel this desire to take the toy, they won't do it because they'll know that they'll be punished for it. So until they get old enough to understand, you can actually, through fear, get someone to do the right thing. There is a certain benefit to that.

Right and Wrong

When our oldest son was just about two years old, we were walking out in the country on a dirt road. The weeds were up around four or five feet high. He was just a tiny little boy, running up about thirty yards ahead of us. We were walking and talking because nobody ever came down this dirt road. But there was an intersection up ahead. And although it was unusual, there was a car coming down that dirt road at fifty or sixty miles per hour. The car was coming so fast that I couldn't have run quickly enough to have physically stopped my son. Joshua reached this intersection at the exact moment that car was whizzing by. The weeds were high and they couldn't see him. They were on a collision course.

But we had been training him to obey us. If he didn't, he got a spanking. So I shouted, "Joshua, stop!" Boy, he froze mid-stride while that car zoomed on by just a few feet away.

Many people don't discipline their kids. They just think they ought to reason with them. They're just making that child susceptible to temptation. They need to learn to do what's right before they reason.

> The natural man receiveth not the things of the Spirit of God: for they are foolishness unto him: neither can he know them, because they are spiritually discerned.
>
> 1 Corinthians 2:14

Before someone is born again, they just don't have the capacity to understand spiritual things. So then, how could God restrict the amount of sin being committed? How could He get us pointed in the right direction and doing the right thing, even though we didn't have the capacity for spiritual understanding before being born again? God had to create the law to teach people right and wrong, by making fear of the consequences if they disobeyed their motivation for obedience.

CHAPTER 18

Old vs. New

There is no fear in love; but perfect love casteth out fear: because fear hath torment. He that feareth is not made perfect in love.

1 John 4:18

In the New Covenant, we aren't supposed to be serving God out of fear of punishment. Yet most people haven't understood this. They're still operating under Old Covenant fear. They're afraid that God is angry with them and that He's imputing sin unto them. This needs to change. That was only a temporary way God dealt with us until we could be born again. Now that we're new creatures in Christ, we have an intuitive knowledge. God is inside us, informing us of right and wrong, and leading us in the way we should go. As a Christian, you don't have to fear the wrath and judgment of God.

I grew up near a busy city street. My dad died when I was a young boy, so my mother raised me. She'd spank me if I ever crossed that street without looking both ways. I received many whippings over that. So here I am, around sixty, and I still look both ways two or three times whenever I cross a street. "Look both ways before you cross the street!" was just drilled into me. Now I understand that it's not the fact my mother will give me a spanking that causes me to do this. I've gone way beyond that. I do what's right, not because I'll get in trouble, but because I don't want to be hit by a car.

What would you think if we were talking, I forgot what I was doing, we crossed a street, then I realized that I didn't look both ways, and said, "Oh no, I didn't look both ways. Please don't tell my mom! She'll give me a whipping"? If I responded that way as an adult, you'd look at me and say, "What's wrong with you?" Mom is currently ninety-five (at the time of this writing). I don't have to be afraid of her spanking me anymore. Now I do what's right, but from a totally different motivation.

Never God's Best

I'm not saying that we no longer do what's right, but the Old Testament law was in place during a brief period of time—until people could be born again—when God used fear, wrath, and punishment to motivate people to live right. Remember, the negative side effect of fear is torment, and the truth is that most people are tormented. They aren't able to enter into the closeness and relationship God desires to have with them, which is the reason that He didn't start imputing man's sins unto them from the very beginning.

If God wanted to just impute man's sins unto them, He could have sat Adam and Eve down and said, "All right, let Me show you what your transgression has just done. Let Me show you what's going to happen in the human race." Just in the past century alone, God could have shown them the world wars, Hitler, Stalin, Pol Pot, and all the people these evil dictators killed.

If He would have just told Adam the heartache, hurt, pain, sickness, disease, anger, bitterness, and all of the other ungodly things that mankind would experience, I don't think Adam could have lived with himself. He wouldn't have been able to handle it. God could have shown him His wrath. He could have shown Adam how bad he was. But the Lord didn't sit him down and say, "Thou shalt not kill, thou shalt not commit adultery," and so on. Why didn't He give the Ten Commandments to Adam and Eve? He was talking to them in an audible voice. It seems as though it would have been a great opportunity to give it to them. Why did He wait another 2,500 years? The reason is that the law was never God's best.

God didn't want us to know the depths of our sin. He didn't want Adam to feel so bad that he ran from Him. God extended mercy to people for 2,500 years, but they were taking His lack of judgment as approval. After Cain got by with murder, his great-great-great-grandson Lamech killed a man in self-defense. Lamech told his wives:

> If Cain shall be avenged sevenfold, truly Lamech seventy and sevenfold.
>
> Genesis 4:24

In other words, "I was more justified in my murder than Cain was. So if God protected Cain, then He has to protect me that much more." They began comparing themselves among themselves and got to where they felt it wasn't wrong to murder people. (See 2 Cor. 10:12.) It wasn't wrong to commit adultery, sexual immorality, or sodomy. (See Eccl. 8:11.) People were losing their standard of right and wrong. God had to do something to impose a standard on people because they didn't know what was right or wrong anymore.

"God Will Accept Me"

The same exact thing has been happening in our society. Fifty years ago, homosexuality was considered wrong. It wasn't accepted, so it wasn't flaunted openly as it is now. Homosexuals didn't have parades and promote themselves as "gay." Then a few rock stars, a politician, and a movie star—with all of their fame and fortune—"came out" as homosexuals, and all of a sudden the world began to feel differently about it. The general public sees those living in this sin who are famous, rich, on the covers of magazines, and respected by the world, so they don't feel as badly about the lifestyle as they once did. But that doesn't change the fact that homosexuality is still as wrong as it ever was, according to the Bible. (See Lev. 18:22; 20:13; Rom. 1:26–28.)

Many people today, though, don't have an absolute standard established in their heart—it's just relative. So they "go with the flow" of the world's standard. Christians try to be a little bit better than the average in our society, but we don't go by what the Word of God says as a whole. That's wrong! We ought to go by what God's Word says. But we're comparing ourselves among ourselves. How did God break that? He established a standard that showed man the wrath of God. Those who had a desire to obey God all of a sudden realized, "If this is what He's demanding, I'm in big trouble!"

One of the main purposes of the law isn't to get you to keep everything in it. If you really study the law, you'll find that it's very detailed. For instance, if you're wearing a garment today that has part wool and part cotton in it, you've broken the law. (See Lev. 19:19.) It's down to some very specific details. The law had requirements for everything, even telling people the proper protocol for going to the bathroom. (See Deut. 23:12–14.)

Some folks tell me, "I believe you have to keep the law." They've come up and criticized me, saying, "I still think we have to keep the Ten Commandments." I have yet to have anybody who's told me that who could give me all ten of the commandments. And there's much more than just ten commandments. There are hundreds of commandments about everything.

Some people who have seen the scriptures about being delivered from the Old Testament law say that it was only the "ceremonial" law that passed away. By *ceremonial*, they mean the feast days, sacrifices, and such. Yet 2 Corinthians 3:7 speaks of the law that was written and engraved in stone passing away. That's referring to the Ten Commandments. These Ten Commandments are still right and holy, but God doesn't relate to us based on our adherence to them anymore. So the scriptures that speak of us being delivered from the law are talking about the whole law—Ten Commandments and ceremonial.

One of the reasons God gave the law was for people who had been comparing themselves among themselves and thinking,

*I'm a pretty good person. I know I'm not everything I should be, but
I'm a relatively good person.* People who believe God grades on a
curve know that He has to accept somebody. Since nobody's
perfect, it doesn't really matter whether you're perfect. It's just
how you are in relation to everyone else. *God will accept me if
I'm in the top ten percentile.* That's the way many people think.

The Standard

Here's what God did for those who were thinking, *Well, I'm
pretty good. I don't dip, cuss, or chew, or go with those who do. At
least I'm not like this publican over here. I fast twice a week.* (See
Luke 18:11–12.) God said, "You think you're good enough? Let
Me show you what real holiness is." Then He gave a standard
that nobody could keep.

The law wasn't really given for you to keep. Now, there is
benefit in keeping it to the degree that you can. This keeps Satan
off your back. But nobody could ever keep the law perfectly—
except Jesus. The law was given to give you such a standard that
it would condemn you.

> The strength of sin is the law.
>
> 1 Corinthians 15:56

> The letter [of the law] killeth.
>
> 2 Corinthians 3:6

The law stops our excuses, makes us guilty, and focuses our
attention on sin. (See Rom. 3:19,20.) It also releases wrath (instead
of mercy) and gives sin dominion over us. (See Rom. 4:15; 6:14.)

I had not known sin, but by the law…. For without the law sin was dead. For I was alive without the law once: but when the commandment came, sin revived, and I died.

Romans 7:7–9

The law wasn't something given to help you. It was given to beat you down and hurt you. It was given to take away your self-righteousness, condemn you, and make you feel unworthy. Basically, it was to knock you flat on your face before God saying, "If this is what You demand, I have no chance. Have mercy on me, a sinner!" The purpose of the law was to drive you to the mercy and grace of God.

"What Makes You Worthy?"

A certain man went to heaven. He was really smug because he'd been a very good person on earth. Peter met him at the pearly gates and asked, "Well, what makes you worthy to enter?"

The man answered, "I'm a really good person."

"Okay. You need a hundred points to get into heaven. Tell me what you've done."

"I went to church every single Sunday. In fact, I had a church attendance award pin for never missing."

"Good! That's worth half a point."

"Half a point!"

"Yes, half a point."

"Well, I was faithful to my wife. I never cheated on her."

"Good! That's worth one point."

Starting to get desperate, he stated, "I tithed to the church all my life, and gave offerings a few times too!"

"That's worth one point."

This man listed four or five different things, but had only accumulated five points. So he threw up his arms in exasperation and exclaimed, "At this rate, I can't get in unless it's by the grace of God!"

"*Bingo!* That's worth one hundred points. Come on in."

That's the purpose of the law. It's for people who were thinking, *I'm pretty good*. You can't get saved trusting in yourself and your own goodness. God had to take away this self-righteousness and get you to recognize that you had to trust in His mercy and grace, not yourself. How did He do it? He gave you such a standard—one through ten thousand things to do—that the purpose was to make you despair of self-righteousness and get you out of thinking you could be good enough on your own. The law made all of us guilty before God. (See Rom. 3:23.) It shuts your mouth and reveals how far you've missed the mark.

The Word of Reconciliation

Religion has made the law out to be something positive. "God loved us so much that He gave us step one through ten thousand to show us exactly what we must do to get right with Him." No, the law was meant to kill. (See 2 Cor. 3:7.) It was meant to destroy. The law was meant to shut you up—make you hopeless and helpless—so that you would cry out to God for mercy. (See Gal. 3:23.) Yet, most of the church has embraced it and wants to promote it. The law was given to kill us. We need to get out from under the law and start relating to God based on His mercy and grace.

So, for those first 2,500 years, God dealt with mankind in mercy. But when people began to take His lack of judgment as approval, He needed to do something. They had lost their concept of right and wrong because they were comparing themselves among themselves. They were getting into self-righteousness, living ungodly, but thinking, *I'm wonderful even though I've done all of these things.* God had to bring an end to that, so He gave the law, started judging people's sins, and began punishing them accordingly.

That put fear in people. It limited the amount of sin they did, but it caused the sin people committed to just destroy them. (See Prov. 16:6.) Instead of enjoying relationship with God, people were living under condemnation. Jesus came to redeem us from that law and condemnation and has put us back into right relationship with the Father. Now we can just love God—and He's not imputing our sins unto us.

> God was in Christ, reconciling the world unto himself, not imputing their trespasses unto them; and hath committed unto us the word of reconciliation. Now then we are ambassadors for Christ, as though God did beseech you by us: we pray you in Christ's stead, be ye reconciled to God.
>
> 2 Corinthians 5:19,20

The Lord has given us this ministry of telling people, "God's not mad at you. He's not angry. He's not imputing your sins unto you." Remember, it's His goodness that leads us to repentance. (See Rom. 2:4.)

Relate by Love

As believers, we need to have enough discernment to know what was Old Testament law and why God gave it, and to recognize that under the New Testament we have a better covenant. We aren't under the Old Testament law anymore. We're under the law of loving God and loving people. Those are the two commandments Jesus gave. He said that if you love God with all your heart, and love your neighbor as yourself, you'll fulfill all of the precepts and ordinances of the Old Testament law. (See Matt. 22:37–40.) In fact, you'll do it better than living out of fear and trying to pay it by debt and obligation.

When I first saw the grace and mercy of God in the New Testament, and the wrath of God in the Old, I couldn't reconcile it. I thought, *Is God schizophrenic? Has He changed? What happened?* God has always been the same. He's always loved us because He is love (see 1 John 4:8).

We had to correct our children for a period of time by spanking them. It wasn't because we hated them. It was that we were trying to get them to do the right thing before they fully understood. But it was just a temporary way of dealing with them. Now that they're adults, we have to release them and deal with them in a different manner. The parent doesn't change, but the child does. So the way the parent deals with the child changes as they grow up. Yet we've always loved them and had their best interests in mind.

Now that we're born again, God isn't imputing our sins unto us. God's not going to "get you." He's not punishing you. God isn't the One who's causing problems in your life. Now you're free to relate to Him based on love. We have a New Covenant—a better covenant. Christ redeemed us from the law. We've been redeemed from the curse of the law (see Gal. 3:13). Isn't that good news?

New Covenant Eyes

Even though the emphasis of my preaching is God's love and grace, I spend most of my time studying the Old Testament. Now that I have this revelation of the New Covenant, I can look back at what I've been redeemed from. I can see how terrible it was when God put wrath and punishment upon people. Even though I deserve those things, God is extending mercy and grace toward me. This makes me love and appreciate Him that much more.

Many Christians have been looking at the New Testament through Old Testament glasses. If you're one of them, know that once you understand these truths, you'll be able to look at the whole of God's Word in proper perspective. You'll start seeing the Old Covenant through New Covenant eyes.

As you see what we've been redeemed from, gratefulness will well up in your heart toward the Lord. You'll find yourself saying, "Thank You, Jesus, for the greater day we live in today."

The body of Christ hasn't been taking advantage of our New Covenant. We've been living as Old Covenant people. We've been living as if Jesus hadn't come and set us free from all of these rituals and legalistic obligations. We need to recognize and receive a revelation of the New Covenant we've been given. We need to get into God's Word to discover what all of our benefits are, and how we can take full advantage of them.

CHAPTER 19

Spiritual Dyslexia

G od has already placed all of our sin upon Jesus. He not only paid for all the sins of believers, but of unbelievers too. Christ paid for all the sins—past, present, and even future sins—of the entire world. Sins have been paid for!

God isn't angry. He's not judging us for our sin. Jesus drew all judgment to Himself at the cross. God is really just dealing with people today based on whether or not they've made Jesus their Lord. It's all a matter of what we do with Jesus.

Remember, people go to hell not because of their individual sins, but because they rejected Jesus. If you've accepted Christ, then you have a relationship with God. All sins—past, present, and even future sins—have been paid for. You're not going to do anything that will surprise the Lord, or that hasn't already been dealt with. Every time you sin, you don't have to go and "get the blood reapplied." You don't have to get that sin confessed and "back under the blood," or you're out of fellowship and relationship with God until you do so. Those things are being taught, but they're not what the Scripture reveals at all.

Understanding that Jesus has suffered for us and paid for all our sin, and that He's not angry with us and He'll never rebuke us again, enables us to enjoy God's love in a much deeper way. When we comprehend how much the Lord loves us, our faith shoots through the roof because faith works by love (see Gal. 5:6). Every area of our life is affected. Basically, this is what the book of 1 John is written about.

Relationship with God

That which was from the beginning, which we have heard, which we have seen with our eyes, which we have looked upon, and our hands have handled, of the Word of life; (for the life was manifested, and we have seen it, and bear witness, and shew unto you that eternal life, which was with the Father, and was manifested unto us;) that which we have seen and heard declare we unto you, that ye also may have fellowship with us: and truly our fellowship is with the Father, and with his Son Jesus Christ. And these things write we unto you, that your joy may be full.

1 John 1:1–4

John was saying, "We're writing this so that you can receive a revelation of Jesus. Then you can have fellowship with both the Father and us. We're writing this so that you can have fellowship with God." This close, intimate relationship with God is actually the true goal and aim of Christianity.

If you really understood how much God loves you, it would just increase your relationship with Him. Then—as you come to know Him more—He'll reveal things to you. Everything in the Christian life flows out of this.

My teaching entitled *Eternal Life* addresses this very topic. If I only had one chance to minister to someone, I'd share with them this message.

John said, "I'm writing this so that you would come into a deeper revelation of God, have fellowship with Him, and your joy would be made full." In both the world and the church, people are trying to find joy in every possible way apart from intimacy with God. However, it's through a vital, growing, daily relationship with Him that joy—and everything else we need—comes. It all boils down to relationship with God.

Seeing Things Backwards

Then John said some things that appear—on the surface—to be contrary to some of these truths I've been emphasizing.

> Hereby we do know that we know him, if we keep his commandments.
>
> 1 John 2:3

A condition exists in the body of Christ today called *spiritual dyslexia*. Dyslexia causes people to see things backwards. To a dyslexic person the word G-O-D is seen as D-O-G. There's a huge difference between *God* and *dog*, but for the dyslexic, everything is reversed in their mind. That is true for spiritual dyslexics as well.

Spiritual dyslexia is contagious. You get it through close contact with religion. It's amazing how people turn these verses in 1 John around and see them as performance-based scripture. People read 1 John 2:3, for instance, and think, *I want to know God, so what do I have to do? I have to keep His commandments. If I keep His commandments, that's how I'll know Him.* That's not what this verse is saying. It's saying the exact opposite. It's not saying that keeping God's commandments will cause you to know Him. It's saying that you can tell if you really know Him because knowing God will cause you to keep His commandments.

If you're truly in fellowship with God—loving Him and His love flowing through you—you'll know because you'll start loving other people.

Communication Isn't the Problem

Most marriage seminars today have totally missed the boat. They emphasize communication, sharing your feelings, and so on. Now don't get me wrong, communication is important. If you never talk to your mate, it'll definitely hinder your relationship. You do need to talk, but that's just dealing with a by-product of the true problem. Communication itself isn't the problem.

People go to these marriage seminars and are taught how to communicate. They're told, "Vent it, let it out, don't hold anything in, talk about it, and get it out." They're even instructed on how to write notes and letters, but all that happens is now they can communicate their anger and hatred that much better.

Many people who have attended my marriage seminars have told me, "Communication nearly killed my marriage!"

Communication isn't the problem; it's just a symptom of the problem. The real problem is that people haven't first of all received the love of God for themselves. They don't know an unconditional love. They think God is just giving them what they deserve, and every time they mess up He rejects them. So people tend to turn around and give to others—especially their spouses—what they have.

You can't give away what you don't have. You can't love other people unconditionally if you haven't first of all received the unconditional love of God. If you ever experience God's unconditional—not based on your performance—love, you'll be able to love your mate unconditionally. If you ever receive a true revelation of God's kind of love, it'll enable you to love your spouse the same way. And when you do love your mate unconditionally, you'll wind up communicating it. Whenever you truly love someone, you communicate it. It's that simple.

Unfortunately, we're teaching communication techniques instead of going to the root of the problem. There is a place for these techniques, but they aren't the root of the problem.

Can You See the Difference?

This is what 1 John 2:3 is talking about. If you want to know, "Do I truly love God? Do I really have His love in me?" you need to check the fruit. (See Gal. 5:22.) God's love in you will cause you to live right and to treat other people right. But for people who suffer from spiritual dyslexia, religion has come in and caused them to think, *Well, I want to know God, so I'm going to try to keep His commandments.* They try to do everything right, thinking that doing so will cause them to love God. But it's just the opposite.

If you aren't loving God, you don't need to start trying to love God and love people better. Instead, you need to say, "God, it's evident that I really don't know Your love for me. If I truly understood how much You love me, I wouldn't treat people like this. If I were in a close relationship with You, I wouldn't be doing these things. Lord, forgive me for not knowing You. Please reveal Yourself to me. Help me to understand, know, and experience Your unconditional love."

If you ever get filled with the love of God, I guarantee that you'll treat other people better. If you aren't keeping the commandments—loving other people—it's because you really don't know God.

> He that saith, I know him, and keepeth not his commandments, is a liar, and the truth is not in him.
>
> 1 John 2:4

People say, "I don't want to be a liar—I want to operate in the truth—so what do I have to do? I have to keep the commandments." No, that's not what this is saying. This is saying that if you profess to know God, but it isn't being manifest through your actions toward other people, then you're just deceiving yourself. Why? Because knowing God—having an intimate relationship with Him—will cause you to love other people. Can you see the difference?

3-D Image

> Whoso keepeth his word, in him verily is the love of God perfected: hereby know we that we are in him.
>
> 1 John 2:5

Many people read this verse and say, "I want God's love perfected, so what I have to do is keep His Word. If I just keep His Word, then the love of God will be perfected in me." No, it's saying just the opposite. If God's love is perfected in you, that will cause you to keep the Word.

If you can see it, this is very simple, but if you can't, it's like one of those 3-D pictures you hang on the wall. On the surface, it just looks like some pattern. But if you stare at it, all of a sudden a 3-D image comes out. Then—once you see it—you can't miss it. But until you see it, you can look at it and miss the true picture.

That's the way it is with these verses. People look at them and they just can't understand. They think 1 John 2:3–5 is saying that we have to keep the commandments so that we can have the love of God. No, it's saying that if we understood the love of God—and had a relationship with Him—that would cause us to keep the commandments. Living holy is a fruit—not a root—of relationship with God. It's a by-product of knowing Him.

So we must receive a revelation of how God loves us unconditionally before we can keep the commandments. Teaching people, "Keep the commandments and then God will love you, accept you, and answer your prayers," is trying to get people to do something they're incapable of doing. You can't give away what you don't have.

Be honest with yourself. Are you suffering from spiritual dyslexia? Have you received a revelation of the unconditional love of God?

CHAPTER 20

Motivated by Love

The Christian life isn't difficult—it's impossible! It is absolutely, physically, humanly impossible.

> But I [Jesus] say unto you, That ye resist not evil: but whosoever shall smite thee on thy right cheek, turn to him the other also. And if any man will sue thee at the law, and take away thy coat, let him have thy cloak also. And whosoever shall compel thee to go a mile, go with him twain [two].
>
> Matthew 5:39–41

That's not just hard to do—it's impossible. Human nature doesn't respond that way. The flesh wants to fight, hurt somebody, or do whatever else it has to do to defend itself. But God has asked us to do things that are absolutely impossible to do.

So, first of all, we must have relationship with God. Then, it's not us living, but Christ living in and through us (see Gal. 2:20).

When you have relationship with God and you understand His perfect love, then you're able to turn around and forgive someone else because you've been forgiven. When you've received His unconditional love, you're able to turn around and love people who don't deserve it because you understand that

God has loved you that way. However, by and large, we haven't been doing this.

Instead, we've been telling people to start doing what's right, "and if you'll do enough good stuff, then God will love you, accept you, and all these things will work." That's impossible. People can't live up to that standard. It drives them away.

Deep Ruts

I talked with a lady recently whose father had raised her in a Pentecostal church. She remembers hearing him speak in tongues. When she received the baptism in the Holy Spirit a short time ago, he was so excited he cried. He had fallen back into drinking, was having problems, and wasn't serving the Lord. She asked me if I knew what to do about it. I don't know all of the reasons, but part of the problem is that he'd been trying to do what is right all of his life and he'd failed.

It's impossible to do right all the time. Everyone fails sometimes, but now he has all of this guilt and condemnation. He's still sensitive to God though. When his daughter received the baptism, tears rolled down his cheeks. He loves God, but he just can't live up to "the standard," so all of that condemnation is just beating him down.

That's not the way the Word of God was intended to operate. The Lord wants us to come into relationship with Him and receive His love. Then, the love of Christ constrains us (see 2 Cor. 5:14). God's love will just flow through us.

I wish I had a better way of making people understand what I'm saying because it's backwards from the way many have thought for so long. We've been taught this so often and so much that it's like going down a dirt road that has ruts so deep you just can't miss them. Every time you go down the road, you just fall into the same old ruts. People just automatically fall into the same thought patterns because it's been said so often, so loud, and so much, but the truth is different than the way most people are thinking today.

"Great Service"

I was genuinely converted as an eight-year-old. The very next day, without me telling them, my classmates discerned the change, and they made fun of me. So, there was immediate fruit of my newfound life in Christ. I know I was genuinely saved. But even though I loved the Lord with all my heart, I fell into this trap of thinking I had to do something to get God to love me. So, I was always doing things. I didn't really have a revelation of God's love for me. I would have said, "God loves me," but I didn't truly understand it. I didn't realize God's love was unconditional, or I wouldn't have always been trying to do something to get Him to love me more.

I "rededicated" myself every time our church had a service. It didn't matter if we had special meetings every night for a week, I'd go forward. If I would have had a "rededicator," I would have worn it out! I was always seeking after God, but I thought I had to do something to get Him to love me.

An introvert by nature, I couldn't look a person in the face and talk to them. When I was a senior in high school, people would walk down the street and say, "Good morning." I'd be two blocks away before I could respond. I just couldn't talk to people.

Even though I was an introvert and had all of these problems, I was told, "You have to do all of these things, and if you'll do enough good things, then God will accept you." So I took the soul-winning courses, psyched myself up, and went out and knocked on doors every Thursday night for "Adult Visitation." I became so zealous that I started a special Tuesday night visitation for the youth on top of that.

At the age of fourteen, I had trained others in soul-winning and was "leading" three or four people "to the Lord" every week. I'd have them repeat a prayer after me. Then I'd go back to church with their "scalp" and show everybody what I did, trying to gain acceptance and approval. I was doing all of this stuff—Tuesday nights, Thursday nights, reading my Bible every day, never missing a church meeting, and so forth—thinking I was doing this "great service" and trying to get God to love me.

Daylight to Dark

Then on March 23, 1968, I had an experience where God revealed His love to me. First of all, He showed me that my self-righteousness and all the things I was taking pride in were an offense to Him. He showed me I was trusting in myself and my own goodness. I honestly thought God was going to kill me. For an hour and a half, I turned myself inside out confessing all my sins and saying, "God, I'm sorry!" I didn't know how bad I was or how much of a religious Pharisee I was. So I repented of all that and honestly expected God to do away with me that night.

When I saw how bad I was, I thought it was the first time God knew about it. Under the logic I had at the time—that He deals with us based on our performance—I deserved to be killed. So I just confessed everything—hoping that if He did get rid of me, that I wouldn't go to hell, but to heaven instead. To my great surprise, after confessing all of that, the love of God just poured out in my life for about four and a half months. I was just gone somewhere—caught up in the love of God. Tangibly, I knew that God loved me. It was awesome!

For the first time, I knew that God's love for me was unconditional. I knew that there was nothing I did to deserve it. I knew that there was nothing I could ever do to make God not love me. His love for me was totally disconnected from me, separate from anything I deserved. The only thing I had to do was either receive it or reject it, but God loved me passionately, completely separate from anything I deserved.

When I saw that, it didn't make me want to serve God less. I did quit both the Tuesday and Thursday night visitations, though, because I realized that even though I was making several visits a week inviting people to church, I was still letting hundreds of people pass me by every day. So I quit going out special on Tuesday and Thursday nights, and I just started talking to everything that moved. I witnessed daylight to dark. I was knocking on a hundred doors a day!

At one time, I actually made a commitment that I would never see a person whom I wouldn't talk to about Jesus. I kept that up for nearly a year. Finally, I was drafted into the army during Vietnam. I remember standing at attention and seeing hundreds of people march by, and I couldn't talk to them. I thought, *God, I'm going to have to renege on this because I just can't feasibly do it.* But for nearly a year, I talked to everyone I could.

We'd go into a restaurant, and I'd stand up and pray over everybody's food at the top of my lungs. They'd look at me and I'd say, "You need your food blessed too!" I was obnoxious, but I saw people born again doing that. I'd see them coming out of a convenience store with a pack of cigarettes or some liquor, and I'd tell them, "You're going to hell. You need to repent!" It was legalism, but it was motivated by love. I just didn't know any other way to do it. That's the way everybody I was exposed to did it.

Same Action, Different Motive

Instead of feeling like I had to try to do something to get God's love, now I understood that He loved me. So instantly I started sharing with people. I began witnessing to folks. I just gave my life trying to share this love with other people. If you really know how much God loves you, you will truly fall in love with Him and nobody will have to preach to you about going out and sharing your faith.

Many pastors have trouble motivating the people in their church to evangelize. They will tell their congregation, "Why don't you share your faith? Why don't you talk to people at work? Why don't you tell others about God?" That's just a symptom of a problem. The problem is that the congregation hasn't really received the love of God. They don't truly know how much He loves them. If they knew, they wouldn't be able to keep their mouths shut!

Some pastors try to use condemnation and say things like, "If you don't witness, someday you'll stand before God without any stars in your crown, and you'll be embarrassed." That will cause people to go out and start knocking on doors, not because they love others, but because they love themselves. They don't want to be embarrassed. Since they're doing it out of fear and condemnation, their "witness" comes across like a sounding brass and a tinkling cymbal (see 1 Cor. 13:1). There's no love in it.

People get offended and turned off because of the "religious fanatics" out there saying, "Repent or else. Turn or burn!" Most of them aren't really fanatics. The problem is that they aren't "witnessing" motivated by love. They're doing it trying to obtain God's love and earn His favor.

We need to tell people about the love of God. We need to let them know how good He is. If they ever received a revelation of that, they'd go tell everyone. The issue is motivation. We're trying to get people to do the same action, but from totally different motivations.

Old or New?

Brethren, I write no new commandment unto you, but an old commandment which ye had from the beginning. The old commandment is the word which ye have heard from the beginning. Again, a new commandment I write unto you, which thing is true in him and in you: because the darkness is past, and the true light now shineth.

1 John 2:7,8

This sounds a little bit confusing. John said, "This isn't a new commandment. It's the old commandment—the same thing you've heard from the beginning." Then he turned right around and said, "It's a new commandment." Which is it? Is it an old commandment or a new one? It's both.

What he meant is, none of the rules have changed. It's not that you aren't supposed to love the Lord, worship God, study the Word, pray, and seek Him. It's not that you aren't supposed to love people and treat them right. It's the same thing the Old Testament said, but now it's a different motivation. Therefore, it's a brand-new commandment because instead of commanding you to do all these things, God is saying, love Him and love people. As you do, you'll automatically do these other things.

You'd never lie to someone you truly loved. When you lie, you are manipulating that person. You are changing the facts and taking advantage of them. You would never lie to someone you truly loved because it's making that person act on false information. It'll make a fool out of them. You're taking advantage of them. When you lie, you are operating in nothing but

188

self-love. You don't care about the other person. You're just going to do what it takes to take advantage of them.

If you really loved someone else, you wouldn't steal from them. If you ever steal from somebody—whether it's your boss or your parents, your friend or a stranger—it means that you don't give a rip about them. You don't know what their situation is, and you don't care. You just want something and you're going to take it. All you're doing is thinking about yourself. All thievery is total self-love. It's not loving other people.

Receive God's Love

If you truly loved other people, you'd never gossip about them. You'd never say things behind their back that could hurt them. If you did and they found out what you said, you probably would be ashamed all of a sudden and not want to say it anymore, but not because you care anything about them. People who gossip care only about themselves, and they say anything that advantages them, anything they feel like. Gossipers just don't care about other people. The only time it would bother them is if it's going to cost them something, or make them look bad.

If we really loved people, we wouldn't gossip, steal, lie, or treat them the way that we do. If we truly loved God, church leaders wouldn't have to force us to study the Word, meet with other believers, or anything else. The bottom line is that we're still telling people, "You need to love God and do all of these things."

Yet, we have a brand-new motivation. I'm not telling people that we shouldn't be serving God and sharing Jesus with others. I'm just saying that first of all you need to receive the love of God for yourself. You need to understand that the Lord isn't going to love you more if you do everything right, and He's not going to love you less if you do everything wrong. If you could ever get a revelation of that and receive the love of God, His love would cause you to live holy.

CHAPTER 21

God Looks at the Heart

Beloved, let us love one another: for love is of God; and every one that loveth is born of God, and knoweth God.

1 John 4:7

Some people who read this verse say, "Well, I want to be born of God and know God, so what do I have to do? I have to love everybody else." No, this is saying the opposite. It's saying that if you know God, then you'll be born of God and you will love other people. Keeping the commandments and doing these things is the by-product of—not the way to—relationship with God.

He that loveth not knoweth not God; for God is love.

1 John 4:8

You may be one who says of this verse, "Well, I want to know God, so what do I have to do? I have to love other people." No, this is saying the opposite. It's saying that if you would just understand God's love for you and come to know Him, then you would wind up loving other people because God is love. If you're filled with God, you'll be filled with love. Isn't that simple?

Receive First, Then Give

In this was manifested the love of God toward us, because that God sent his only begotten Son into the world, that we might live through him. Herein is love, not that we loved God, but that he loved us, and sent his Son to be the propitiation for our sins.

1 John 4:9,10

What a great truth. You don't first of all love God, and then He loves you back. God loved us first! You must first of all receive the love of God—then you can love God and love others.

You can't give away what you don't have. You can't treat other people right if you think God is treating you wrong. If you think God is dealing with you based on your performance, you'll wind up reproducing that same thing and give other people what they deserve. You'll be as mean as a snake.

I heard about someone recently who had gone through some kind of religious school. They turned from a sweet person into a mean person. That's what religion does because that's what they're teaching that God is—"God is a harsh God."

At some Bible colleges, if men don't wear sleeves down to their wrist, they're "going to hell." One school I know of would kick a person out for wearing a crimson shirt because it's "the color of the beast." That's just legalism. God isn't mad at you because of the way you dress.

Hair, Jewelry, and Makeup

People who say, "You can't wear any makeup, or put on any jewelry," base it on 1 Peter 3, which says:

> Whose adorning let it not be that outward adorning of plaiting the hair, and of wearing of gold.
>
> 1 Peter 3:3

They say, "You shouldn't fix your hair fancy or wear any gold like jewelry." Well, if they would just keep reading, this verse goes on to say:

> Or of putting on of apparel.
>
> 1 Peter 3:3

Does that mean we aren't supposed to wear clothes? Of course not! This whole passage is simply emphasizing, "Don't put your focus on the outward part."

I've seen Pentecostal women before who put on five layers of powder so it wouldn't look like they had rosy cheeks. Since their cheeks were naturally rosy, they went to all of this effort just to look bland and ugly. Personally, I believe that if your barn needs painting, paint it. If it needs two coats, give it two coats! But that's not what this passage is talking about.

A Holy Life

> Beloved, if God so loved us, we ought also to love one another. No man hath seen God at any time. If we love one another, God dwelleth in us, and his love is perfected in us.
>
> 1 John 4:11,12

If you're thinking, *Well, I want God to dwell in me and His love to be perfected, so what do I have to do? We have to love each other!* No, this is saying just the opposite. If you would receive the unconditional love of God, and let that love dwell in you, you'll wind up loving other people automatically.

> Hereby know we that we dwell in him, and he in us, because he hath given us of his Spirit. And we have seen and do testify that the Father sent the Son to be the Saviour of the world. Whosoever shall confess that Jesus is the Son of God, God dwelleth in him, and he in God. And we have known and believed the love that God hath to us. God is love; and he that dwelleth in love dwelleth in God, and God in him.
>
> 1 John 4:13–16

We could just go on and on with this. If you don't understand what I'm talking about, the book of 1 John will look like you have to do these things and then God responds. But it's actually saying just the opposite. It's saying that if you truly knew God, you would wind up living a holy life.

Actions Are Evidence

Living holy doesn't earn us favor with God, but it does evidence His presence in our life. Someone may come to me and say, "Oh yeah, I know God. He and I are tight. I fellowship with Him and love Him with all of my heart. We're best friends!" Yet they don't trust God in their giving; they are lying, stealing, and committing adultery—and I'm not talking about an isolated instance. It's their lifestyle. If they're just living like the devil—

they can say whatever they want, but I don't believe it. Those things don't reflect God in a person's life.

"But, Andrew, isn't that undoing everything you've said?" No, it's a perfect balance. Our holiness doesn't make God love us. But if God's love is dwelling in us, and we're dwelling in it, His love will cause us to live holy. "Living holy" doesn't mean that you'll live by all the principles and standards of some religious sect. Everything they say is "holy" isn't necessarily holy. But God's love will cause you to love Him and love people.

If you say, "I really do know God. We have a great relationship," yet you're as mean as a snake—you don't love others, you never do anything for anyone, you don't think about anybody else beside yourself, you can see people in need and not even care—confess what you will, but the Word of God says:

> Whoso hath this world's good, and seeth his brother have need, and shutteth up his bowels of compassion from him, how dwelleth the love of God in him?
>
> 1 John 3:17

You can say that you love God, but the truth is you can tell by your actions whether His love is really dwelling in you or not.

Religion or True Christianity?

Instead of thinking, *I have to earn the blessing of God by doing these things*, you need to recognize that living properly, treating other people right, loving your mate, and so forth are all byproducts of relationship with God. If you have a temper, and you fly off the handle, don't say, "O God, help me quit this!" and start trying to treat other people right so that God will love you. Instead, reverse it and say, "Father, I recognize that the reason I'm like this is because I don't really know You. I haven't really received Your love. I'm just treating people the way I think You are treating me. Lord, I need a revelation of Your love for me!" If you would take the truths we've talked about in this study—that all of your sins have been paid for, that God's not angry with you, and so on—and meditate on them, the Lord would reveal His love to you. Once you fall in love with God and His love begins to flow in your life, it'll cause you to live holy. You will have your "fruit unto holiness, and the end everlasting life" (Rom. 6:22).

Holiness is the fruit—not the root—of salvation. This is where religion has gone wrong.

Man looketh on the outward appearance, but the LORD looketh on the heart.

1 Samuel 16:7

This is one way you can tell if it's religion or true Christianity. Religion always focuses on the external person. They're always trying to get you to clean up the outside—fix this and quit doing that—because that's what mankind looks at and deals with. They don't really care about the heart. As long as you come to church, pay your tithes, and dress the way they want you to when you're there, they don't care what you do during the week. It doesn't matter if your heart is right or not. Religion just deals with the external, but God deals with the heart.

The Lord wants to come in, touch your heart, and reveal His love to you. If that ever happens, the rest will be taken care of.

Short Shorts and Halter Tops

Jamie and I pastored this little church in Childress, Texas for a while. One day, we took a small group out to the park for a picnic. While there, we came across a family—a husband, wife, and their two-year-old daughter—who had been living out of the back of their pickup. It turned out that they had just left the nudist colony where they had been living for the past three years. They were totally broke and had run out of gas in this city park where we were having our picnic. So they came over and begged us for some food.

We gave them something to eat and began sharing the Gospel with them. They hadn't taken a bath in days, so some of our people opened up their home and started helping them get cleaned up, gave them some clothes, and other things they needed. Anyway, we led this couple to the Lord and they became born again. So they started coming to church.

Now this woman was well endowed and nice looking. Since they'd been in a nudist colony for so long, all she had to wear was short shorts and halter tops. That's all she had, so that's what she came to church in. We sat in a semicircle during the services so you couldn't avoid looking at her because we were all facing each other. During praise and worship, she'd go to bouncing, jumping, and praising God. It just left little to the imagination.

This was causing some problems with the other people in the church, so several of them came to me demanding, "Aren't you going to tell her that she needs to put some clothes on?" I answered, "We didn't tell her that before she became born again. We didn't throw a sheet over her and tell her that God wouldn't save her if she didn't put some clothes on. Give her some time. She just became born again. Let her enjoy the fact that God loves her. He'll show her some things. But in the meantime, I'm not going to sit there and condemn her."

So we allowed this woman to keep coming to church. Not too long after that, she came to one of Jamie's Bible studies. The woman stood up and told these ladies, "I have never owned a dress in all of my life. I would really like to have a dress. Would you all pray with me?" They not only prayed with her, but within an hour after that Bible study she had a dozen dresses that were all up to her neck and all the way down to the floor. She came to church that night showing off her dress and just praising God. "Look what the Lord did!" She never had anyone tell her, "God's angry with you. He doesn't love you because of the way you dress." It worked out.

Now, most people would sit there and say, "Cover up!" instead of just letting God love her and speak to her over time. She and her husband had just been miraculously saved. Although great things were happening, it takes a little while to turn your whole life around. Religion just wants to deal with the external. We want to put them into our clothes, make them as drab as we are, and make them over into what we think they should be so that we feel better. But we don't care what's going on in their heart. The Lord isn't like that.

God was more pleased with that woman coming to church in her short shorts and halter top than many Christians who have never dressed that way. Why? Her heart was right. She was in love with Jesus and worshiping Him. God looked at her heart and said, "Awesome!"

"God Is the Best Blankety-Blank!"

One time while I was preaching in Phoenix, a woman in the audience was so excited she was literally bouncing up and down on the front row. Between sessions, I went over and talked to her. She'd just been born again a little over a month, so I asked her to come up and give her testimony.

She stood up in front of the group, and every third or fourth word was profanity. She blasted, cursed, and damned everything. She said words I didn't even know! She was just up there talking about, "God is the best blankety-blank thing that's ever happened to me. This beats sex! This beats drugs!" She was just saying things that would make a sailor turn red.

When the people started reacting, she looked at me and asked, "Am I saying something wrong?"

I answered, "Nope. You're doing great!" So she finished her testimony.

People came up to me afterwards and said, "Why didn't you tell her to stop and not do that?" Again, that's just religion. I'm not saying that we should use profanity, but God was looking at her heart and she didn't realize that Christians didn't talk that way. When I went back there the next year, this woman came up to me and said, "I'm so sorry! I was just born again and I didn't know Christians didn't talk that way. I thought everybody talked that way!" She had learned.

God was more pleased with that woman testifying about how good He is, even though she was using profanity, than He is with many Christians who would never use that terminology. They may have the right religious form, but they don't know Him. They aren't excited about Him. God looks at your heart!

CHAPTER 22

Receive His Love

When you see someone fall in love with God, don't try to squelch that and put them into your religious form. Just encourage them in the love of God. His love will cause them to start keeping the commandments.

We just have it all wrong. We need to change our mindset. If you're sinning, it's because the love of God isn't flowing through you. If you're committing adultery, for instance, don't just sit there and say, "Oh, God, help me to quit operating in lust so I can start getting my prayers answered." That's totally wrong. If you're operating in lust, it's because you don't love God with all of your heart, and you aren't loving your mate. If you were, then you'd never do anything to hurt them. You aren't receiving and giving God's love.

Certain segments of the body of Christ are really big into so-called "accountability groups." You meet together with other people who struggle with the same problem for the purpose of holding each other "accountable." Basically, somebody's checking up on you. If you would lie to God, if you were going to sneak around and try to do something behind His back, you'll find a way to beat that accountability group. This type of group may be a factor—something in your line of defense—but it shouldn't be your first line of defense.

What ought to keep you on the straight and narrow is your own personal relationship with God. It ought to be the fact that He loves you.

Joseph

No doubt you're familiar with the story of Joseph and how his brothers sold him into slavery out of jealousy. (See Gen. 37:25–28.) Potiphar ended up buying him and later, when Potiphar's wife pressed Joseph to commit adultery with her, Joseph said:

> How then can I do this great wickedness, and sin against God?
>
> Genesis 39:9

Joseph didn't consider whether he'd get caught or not. He didn't think about how much he had suffered. After all he'd been through, it would have been easy to rationalize and say, "I deserve to indulge myself this time," but he didn't. Joseph had a personal relationship with God. That's what kept him straight.

This is what's missing in many people's lives. We have a system of rules, and we're doing all of these things. We're practicing "behavior modification." You may be trying to quit smoking, drinking, or some other bad habit, thinking that doing so will make you accepted with God. Yet, the problem is that in your heart you just haven't understood how much God loves you. You haven't been enjoying Him. If you truly fell in love with God, you'd find that these other things would just fall by the wayside.

God loves you independent of your performance. If you ever really received a revelation of that, and knew it, you'd be so thankful that God Almighty—the only One who really has a right to hate you—loves you. If you received a revelation of His unconditional love, you would fall so head over heels in love with Him that you'd give up bubble gum if you thought that would please Him. You'd do anything. It wouldn't matter. Instead of saying, "How little do I have to do to be able to get God to answer my prayer?" it'd be just the opposite. You'd be serving the Lord with your whole heart.

The First Step

God loves us! If we were preaching the love of God, people would be laying down their lives for Him because of love. Love is a greater motivation than fear. You don't need to be afraid, wondering, *What's going to happen if I just start loving God? Will I just go out and commit sin?* No, you'll wind up serving God more accidentally than you ever have on purpose.

A friend of mine in Chicago started preaching on God's love and grace not long ago, saying, "You just need to love God. He's not mad at you. For instance, you don't go to hell for smoking." That really upset several of the elders in the church. Within a couple of weeks, some of the people in the congregation began standing on the doorstep smoking as people came in and out of church. So the elders came to the pastor and said, "See what your preaching has done? Now they're standing out there smoking because you're saying that God loves them whether they smoke or not."

Wisely, he answered, "Go ask if any of them have started smoking since I began preaching this." Not a single one of them had. What happened was they just quit being hypocritical about it. They stopped trying to hide it behind breath mints, hoping that nobody could tell that they had been smoking. This was their first step toward getting free.

I'm not advocating that we change the standards. It's not a new commandment. It's the same thing, but it's a new method. Instead of telling people to quit those things so that God will love them, tell them, "God loves you in spite of who you are, not because of who you are." Let them know about the love of God, and the love of God will cause them to start living holy. It will inspire and empower them to begin doing the right things.

That's what Jesus did. He embraced people who were harlots, tax collectors, and thieves—people who were rejected by the religious system. If Jesus were here today, I believe He would do just like He did in Bible times. The religious leaders would persecute Him and the religious people would crucify Him. Jesus wouldn't last three years in today's religious system. They'd crucify Him in a much shorter period of time. Why? Because Jesus loved people totally independent of their performance. Then He made covenant with them—not based on their actions, but based on whether or not they received His love.

The church has been preaching the wrong message. Mankind tends to look on the flesh and judge people by their actions and outward appearance. We need to start operating in the Spirit and loving people unconditionally. But you can't give away what you don't have. First of all, you need to receive God's unconditional love for yourself.

He Wants to Set You Free

Have you been suffering from spiritual dyslexia? Are you trying to overcome some specific problem so that God will love you? Or are you saying in your heart, "Lord, I need to know Your love for me. I need a spiritual revelation—not just a goose bump or a feeling. God, I want to see Your love for me!"

Once you see that love, it'll transform your life. That's how it happened for me.

Are you saying, "Lord, I've been going about this all wrong; I've been trying to change from the outside in, instead of the inside out"? Is the Holy Spirit showing you that you need a revelation of the love of God? If so, it's because He wants to set you free.

Be honest with yourself. If you can say, "I don't have a revelation of God's love; I need a total transformation; I need to be healed of this spiritual dyslexia and receive a revelation of God's love," then I want to lead you in a prayer. God wants to do a miracle in your heart right now. He wants to transform you from the inside out.

When you receive a spiritual revelation of God's unconditional love, and start walking in it, your actions will change. God's love will set you free from things. Perfect love always casts out fear (see 1 John 4:18).

Open Your Heart

God touched my life and transformed me. Since He's no respecter of persons, He wants to reveal to you the same unconditional love that He's revealed to me. You just have to open up your heart and receive.

I encourage you to pray this out loud right now:

Father, my focus has been on the outside. I've been trying to stop all of these actions and clean myself up in order for You to love me. But now I see that it's not this way at all. It's just a matter of receiving Your love. Father, I want to know You. I desire to receive a spiritual revelation of Your love. Your Word says that the Holy Spirit will teach me all things, lead me into all truth, and bring all things to my remembrance that Jesus has spoken to me. Right now, I believe that You are revealing Yourself to me through the Holy Spirit. By faith, I receive Your unconditional love.

Father, I ask You to break these feelings of guilt, shame, confusion, and condemnation that a works mentality has produced on the inside of me. Thank You for showing me Your supernatural love. Right now, I believe that a seed is being planted in me that will grow. As I meditate on these truths from Your Word, they are going to become a deeper conviction, a deeper revelation of Your unconditional love for me. I thank You that it's Your love that will cause me to start living right. It's Your love that will break these bondages in my life. I receive Your love. Thank You, Jesus!

Have other people hurt you? Have you been abused? Are you transposing those things onto God, thinking that He treats you the same way these people have? That's wrong. It's irrational for you to be mad at God for the way other people have treated you. God isn't like that. He doesn't control all of those things. God is a good God. He's been faithful to you. God has never failed you!

Now pray:

Father, You've been faithful to me. You've been good to me. Please forgive me for swallowing the devil's lie that You love me only when I'm lovely, only when I've done things right. Forgive me for not searching this out in Your Word and for allowing myself to be deceived. I believe that You are setting me free from all religious bondage. I am beginning to experience Your unconditional love right now. I break these religious strongholds that have exalted themselves against the knowledge of You in my life. I release my spiritual weapons and cast that junk down. I take every thought captive and bring them under obedience to Christ.

Here's one more thing I'd like you to pray:

Father, I thank You that these truths will be brought back to my remembrance by the Holy Spirit. Your Word is going to burn on the inside of me until it cleans out all of this wrong thinking and I come to know You intimately as the good, merciful, kind heavenly Father that You are. You placed all of the judgment I deserved upon Jesus. You aren't angry with me. You aren't disappointed with me. The war is over. Your anger against my sin is satisfied. You rejected Your own Son so that You would never reject me. Thank You for loving me. I receive Your love!

I encourage you to spend some time right now just praising and worshiping the Lord. Let His unconditional love overwhelm you. Enjoy His awesome presence. Relationship with God is what you were created for!

Progressive Revelation

What you're receiving is a progressive revelation. Although I had that encounter with the Lord on March 23, 1968, I've grown tremendously in what God has done since then. I had an emotional experience, but emotions don't last forever. If I hadn't received the truth, begun to meditate on it, and learned these things, I would have long since lost that experience. It's the truth you know and have established in your heart that sets you free (see John 8:32). It doesn't matter how you feel. You could minister this truth to yourself and control your emotions. You can learn to enjoy the presence of God even without a goose bump. The love of God isn't a feeling. It's a revelation. That revelation can produce feelings, but feelings come and go. Thank God, the revelation doesn't.

If you prayed that prayer in faith, something has definitely begun. Go to the Word of God. Start praying and seeking Him. Meditate on these truths, and the Lord will continue revealing His love to you. He's promised that when you seek Him with all your heart, you will find Him. (See Jer. 29:13.) "God is love" (1 John 4:8.) He longs to reveal Himself to you, and draw you into a deeper relationship with Him. Praise God, the war is over!

Receive Jesus as Your Savior

Choosing to receive Jesus Christ as your Lord and Savior is the most important decision you'll ever make!

God's Word promises, "If thou shalt confess with thy mouth the Lord Jesus, and shalt believe in thine heart that God hath raised him from the dead, thou shalt be saved. For with the heart man believeth unto righteousness; and with the mouth confession is made unto salvation.... For whosoever shall call upon the name of the Lord shall be saved" (Rom. 10:9,10,13).

By His grace, God has already done everything to provide salvation. Your part is simply to believe and receive.

Pray out loud, *Jesus, I confess that You are my Lord and Savior. I believe in my heart that God raised You from the dead. By faith in Your Word, I receive salvation now. Thank You for saving me!*

The very moment you commit your life to Jesus Christ, the truth of His Word instantly comes to pass in your spirit. Now that you're born again, there's a brand-new you!

Receive the Holy Spirit

As His child, your loving heavenly Father wants to give you the supernatural power you need to live this new life.

For every one that asketh receiveth; and he that seeketh findeth; and to him that knocketh it shall be opened... If ye...know how to give good gifts unto your children: how much more shall your heavenly Father give the Holy Spirit to them that ask him?

Luke 11:10,13

All you have to do is ask, believe, and receive!

Pray, *Father, I recognize my need for Your power to live this new life. Please fill me with Your Holy Spirit. By faith, I receive it right now! Thank You for baptizing me. Holy Spirit, You are welcome in my life.*

Congratulations! Now you're filled with God's supernatural power. Some syllables from a language you don't recognize will rise up from your heart to your mouth. (See 1 Cor. 14:14.) As you speak them out loud by faith, you're releasing God's power from within and building yourself up in the spirit. (See 1 Cor. 14:4.) You can do this whenever and wherever you like.

It doesn't really matter whether you felt anything or not when you prayed to receive the Lord and His Spirit. If you believed in your heart that you received, then God's Word promises you did. "Therefore I say unto you, What things soever ye desire, when ye pray, believe that ye receive them, and ye shall have them" (Mark 11:24). God always honors His Word; believe it!

Please contact me and let me know that you've prayed to receive Jesus as your Savior or to be filled with the Holy Spirit. I would like to rejoice with you and help you understand more fully what has taken place in your life. I'll send you a free gift that will help you understand and grow in your new relationship with the Lord. Welcome to your new life!

We Would Like to Hear From You

If you have prayed the salvation prayer for the first time, or if you have a testimony to share after reading this book, please send us an email at www.harrisonhouse.com.

Or you may write to us at:

Harrison House Publishers

P.O. Box 35035

Tulsa, Oklahoma 745153

www.harrisonhouse.com

Endnotes

Chapter 1

[1] Based on information from Thayer and Smith, *The KJV New Testament Greek Lexicon,* "Greek Lexicon entry for Euaggelizo," available from http://www.biblestudytools.net/Lexicons/Greek/grk.cgi?number=2097&version=kjv, s.v. "gospel," Matthew 11:15.

[2] Ibid., "Greek Lexicon entry for Soteria," available from http://www.biblestudytools.net/Lexicons/Greek/grk.cgi?number=4991&version=kjv, s.v. "salvation," Romans 1:16.

[3] "As there is an absolute necessity that a child should be born into the world, that he may see its light, contemplate its glories, and enjoy its good, so there is an absolute necessity that the soul should be brought out of its state of darkness and sin, through the light and power of the grace of Christ, that it may be able to see,...to discern, the glories and excellencies of the kingdom of Christ here," Adam Clarke, *The Adam Clarke Commentary,* "Commentary on John 3," available from http://www.studylight.org/com/acc/view.cgi?book=joh&chapter=003, s.v. "born again," John 3:3.

[4] Based on information from *Noah Webster's Dictionary of American English,* available from http://www.e-sword.net/dictionaries.html, s.v. "impute," 2 Corinthians 5:19.

Chapter 4

[1] Controversial novel questioning the authenticity of Christianity and the New Testament's account of Jesus' life.

Chapter 6

[1] Thayer and Smith, "Greek Lexicon entry for Katakrino," available from http://www.biblestudytools.net/Lexicons/Greek/grk.cgi?number=2632&version=kjv, s.v. "condemned," Romans 8:3.

Chapter 7

[1] Thayer and Smith, "Greek Lexicon entry for Soteria," available from http://www.biblestudytools.net/Lexicons/Greek/grk.cgi?number=4991&version=kjv, s.v. "salvation," Romans 1:16.

[2] Ibid., "Greek Lexicon entry for Sozo," available from http://www.biblestudytools.net/Lexicons/Greek/grk.cgi?number=4982&version=kjv, s.v. "save," James 5:15.

Chapter 9

[1] Based on information from Thayer and Smith, "Greek Lexicon entry for Prosagoge," available from http://www.biblestudytools.net/Lexicons/Greek/grk.cgi?number=4318&version=kjv, s.v. "access," Romans 5:2; and "Greek Lexicon entry for Prosago,' available from http://www.biblestudytools.net/Lexicons/Greek/grk.cgi?number=4317&version=kjv.

Chapter 14

[1] Based on information from Brown, Driver, Briggs, and Gesenius, *The KJV Old Testament Hebrew Lexicon,* "Hebrew Lexicon entry for Shuwb," available from http://www.biblestudytools.net/Lexicons/Hebrew/heb.cgi?number=7725&version=kjv, s.v. "repent," 1 Kings 8:47.

Chapter 15

[1] Fritz Rienecker, *Linguistic Key to the Greek New Testament* (Grand Rapids, Michigan: Zondervan Publishing House), 1976, 1980; p. 785, s.v. "1 John 1:7."

[2] Ibid., p. 786, s.v. "1 John 1:9."

Chapter 16

[1] Pol Pot was prime minister of Cambodia from 1976 to 1979 and leader of the Communist movement there called the Khmer Rouge. Under his evil leadership close to a million people in his country died.

[2] The Ugandan dictator who took power in the early 1970s and ruled as president of Uganda until 1979. It is estimated that hundreds of thousands of people died under his ruthless leadership during that time.

About the Author

For over three decades Andrew Wommack has traveled America and the world teaching the truth of the Gospel. His profound revelation of the Word of God is taught with clarity and simplicity, emphasizing God's unconditional love and the balance between grace and faith.

He reaches millions of people through the daily *Gospel Truth* radio and television programs, broadcast both domestically and internationally. He founded Charis Bible College in 1994 and has since established CBC extension schools in other major cities of America and around the world.

Andrew has produced a library of teaching materials—available in print, audio, and visual formats. And, as it has been from the beginning, his ministry continues to distribute free audio tapes and CDs to those who cannot afford them.

To contact Andrew Wommack please write, email, or call:

Andrew Wommack Ministries
P.O. Box 3333 • Colorado Springs, CO 80934-3333
Email: awommack@aol.com
Helpline Phone (orders and prayer): 719-635-1111
Hours: 4:00 am to 9:30 pm MST

Andrew Wommack Ministries of Europe
P.O. Box 4392 • WS1 9AR Walsall • England
Email: enquiries@awme.net
U.K. Helpline Phone (orders and prayer):
011-44-192-247-3300
Hours: 5:30 am to 4:00 pm GMT

Or visit him on the web at:
www.awmi.net

Discover the Keys to Staying Full of God

Do you feel as if your Christian life is full of highs and lows? Perhaps you attend a special church service that draws you close to God or even experience a healing. In those moments your heart is filled with the presence of God, but within a few days or weeks, you once again feel empty or sick. You are not alone. Even though many believers experience this, it is not what the Lord intended.

The keys to staying full of God are not a secret and they are not mysterious, they are simple. For that very reason few people recognize their value and even less practice them! In this amazingly practical message, Andrew Wommack reveals the essentials to a strong, close relationship with God. Learn what they are and how to put them into practice. It will keep your heart sensitive toward God and your relationship will grow like never before!

Item Code: 1029-C   4-CD album

ISBN: 1-57794-934-X Paperback

Available at bookstores everywhere
or visit **www.harrisonhouse.com**

Grace, The Power of the Gospel

Recent surveys indicate that the vast majority of Christians, those claiming to be born-again, believe that their salvation is at least in part dependent upon their behavior and actions. Yes, they believe Jesus died for their sin, but once they accept Him as their Savior they believe they must still meet a certain standard to be "good" enough.

If that is true, then what is that standard and how do you know when you have met it? The Church has tried to answer these questions for centuries and it always results in religious and legalistic bondage.

So what is the answer? It begins by asking the right question. It is not, "What must we do?" but rather, "What did Jesus do?" By understanding the Apostle Paul's revelation of what Jesus did from the book of Romans, you will never again wonder if you're meeting the standard.

Item Code: 1014-C   4-CD album

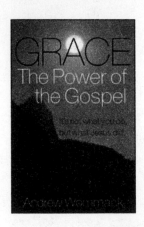

ISBN: 1-57794-921-8 Paperback

Available at bookstores everywhere
or visit **www.harrisonhouse.com**

Other Teachings by Andrew Wommack

Spirit, Soul & Body

Understanding the relationship of your spirit, soul, and body is foundational to your Christian life. You will never truly know how much God loves you or believe what His Word says about you until you do. In this series, learn how they're related and how that knowledge will release the life of your spirit into your body and soul. It may even explain why many things are not working the way you had hoped.

Item Code: 318   Paperback
Item Code: 1027-C   4-CD album

The True Nature of God

Are you confused about the nature of God? Is He the God of judgment found in the Old Testament or the God of mercy and grace found in the New Testament? Andrew's revelation on this subject will set you free and give you a confidence in your relationship with God like never before. This is truly nearly-too-good-to-be-true news.

Item Code: 308   Paperback
Item Code: 1002-C   5-CD album

Living in the Balance of Grace and Faith

This book explains one of the biggest controversies in the church today. Is it grace or faith that releases the power of God? Does God save people in His sovereignty, or does your faith move Him? You may be surprised by the answers as Andrew reveals what the Bible has to say concerning these important questions and more. This will help you receive from God in a greater way and will change the way you relate to Him.

Item Code: 301B   Paperback

The Believer's Authority

Like it or not, every one of us is in a spiritual war. You can't be discharged from service, and ignorance of the battlefield only aids the enemy. In war, God is always for us, and the devil is against us; whichever one we cooperate with will win. And there's only one way the enemy can get your cooperation—that's through deception. In this teaching, Andrew exposes this war and the enemy for what he is.

Item Code: 1045-C   6-CD album
Item Code: 1045-D   DVD album
                                     (as recorded from television)

The Effects of Praise

Every Christian wants a stronger walk with the Lord. But how do you get there? Many don't know the true power of praise. It's essential. Listen as Andrew teaches biblical truths that will spark not only understanding but will help promote spiritual growth so you will experience victory.

Item Code: 309   Paperback
Item Code: 1004-C   3-CD album

God Wants You Well

Health is something everyone wants. Billions of dollars are spent each year trying to retain or restore health. So why does religion tell us that God uses sickness to teach us something? It even tries to make us believe that sickness is a blessing. That's just not true. God wants you well!

Item Code: 1036-C   4-CD album